SO YOU WANT TO DO A SCIENCE PROJECT!

JOEL BELLER
Assistant Principal—Science
Francis Lewis High School
Flushing, New York

ARCO PUBLISHING, INC.
NEW YORK

507.24

Library of Congress Cataloging in Publication Data
Beller, Joel.
  So you want to do a science project!

  Includes index.
  Summary: A guide to selecting, researching, and
doing science projects—some not too difficult, others
more sophisticated—with lists of projects in various
scientific areas.
  1. Science—Experiments. [1. Science—Experiments.
2. Experiments]   I. Title.
Q182.3.B44   507'.24   81-7943
ISBN 0-668-04987-1   AACR2

Printed in the United States of America

    3 4 5 6 7 8 9 10

Contents

283565

Getting Started

One question that teachers are often asked by their students is "I want to do a science project—can you give me one to do?" Most teachers answer this with a qualified "no." That is to say, all they can do is offer to help you select and plan a project for yourself.

You see, in order to do a science project and really enjoy it—and to really get anything out of it—the idea has to come from you. Especially since you're the one who's going to do the project, not your teacher. And anyway, what kind of science project would you be able to do if your teacher suggested that you find the best conditions for earthworms to reproduce and the first thing you discovered was that you think earthworms are disgusting and slimy and you can't stand the sight of them? So, it's apparent right away that the best course is for you to figure out what you are interested in, find some aspect of that thing that you want to explore, and then go to it.

This book is here to help you do just that. I want to get you started on a project or experiment that is meaningful for you and not beyond your abilities. To do this, the book is divided into three parts. The first part will explain how to select, research and carry out science projects that really aren't too difficult—ones that could be entered in a junior high school or intermediate school Science Fair or one that will just get you a higher grade in Science.

The second section deals with more complicated projects. It details how to plan and carry out a more sophisticated scientific experiment that could be entered in a high school or local Science Fair, or even in the Westinghouse Science Talent Search or other similar science competitions such as SEER (Student Exposition on Energy Resources).

The last part of the book lists and discusses projects that you can do in a number of scientific areas such as biology, chemistry and much, much more.

CHAPTER 1

Why Should I Do a Science Project?

Thousands of science projects are attempted each year by students in the United States and all over the world. Obviously, there must be some benefits one can reap from doing a science project.

In grades seven and eight, or even earlier, you and the rest of your classmates will be told by your teacher, "I want each of you to do a science project. It will be due in a month, just before I make up your report card grades." Classes always greet statements such as this one with groans at the thought of the extra work. Worse yet is the fearful thought, "What shall I do?"

First, you should figure out why your teachers want each of you to carry out a project of some sort. They probably think that by doing a project you will learn more about some particular field of science. Furthermore, your teacher hopes that not only will you become more knowledgable in one area of science, but that you will develop an interest in that area and want to learn more about that particular subject. If you become both knowledgable and interested, it is also possible that you will want to carry on research in that small segment of science in later life. You may continue an investigation started in grade eight through high school, college and beyond. There's even a chance that your research may lead to an important discovery. Maybe you'll be the one to discover how to inexpensively convert coal into gasoline. If that happens, then your science teacher could really be proud since, due to his or her efforts, you were stimulated enough to investigate a scientific problem and came up with an important answer for all of us. And if your becoming a heroic scientist is too much to hope for, then your teachers probably figure that working on an independent project, complete with research, planning, "lab" work and reporting will teach you self-reliance and give you a taste of logical thought. Seems to be a lot of effect for not that much effort, right? Well, you can see that your teacher has much more in mind than just keeping you from watching your favorite TV program when he or she assigns you a science project. Some students even carry out science projects when no teacher has asked them to do one. There are a number of excellent reasons to do this, so let's see what some of their reasons and rewards are.

Some students really enjoy science but don't do too well on written tests for one reason or another. These youngsters realize that one way they can show their teacher that, despite their poor test scores, they are really good science students is by submitting a science project to get a better mark on their report card. After all, the teacher knows that a science project is extra work even if the student is having fun.

Often, high school students who are submitting applications to colleges and universities do an original science investigation. They take on this extra task in order to impress the Admissions Committee of the college where they want to be accepted. Most high schools will note such projects on their permanent records as well as noting participation in a Science Fair or other science competition. Naturally, if you are a winner in the Fair or contest, it is reasonable to assume that you will do well in college... at least in the sciences!

Doing a science project or completing an original experiment also shows that you have initiative and determination, and that you can work independently in a logical and scientific manner. Important, too, is the fact that now your science teacher can write specific comments and compliments about you as a result of the completion of your scientific investigation. Thus recommended, colleges will tend to accept you over other applicants who have not done any independent work.

Another reason for doing a science project is that if you are fortunate enough to be selected as a winner in a regional or national science competition, fame and fortune may come your way. Prizes of cash, scholarships or trips to government or industrial scientific installations are the usual rewards given to winning projects. And besides, the newspapers in your hometown and your local TV station often cover competitions of this sort. Everyone gets a good feeling upon seeing his or her name in print or watching himself talking about his project on the six o'clock news. Even your school newspaper will probably devote some space to you and your award-winning achievements.

Perhaps the best reason of all for doing a science project is the personal satisfaction you get upon completing a task that you have set for yourself, and doing it to the best of your ability—in short, being proud of yourself and of your work! For those of you who choose to plan and carry out an original scientific experiment, there is the added thrill of discovery. You have, by following the scientific method, discovered something that was never known before. This places you among the ranks of other working scientists throughout this country and the world.

And it doesn't matter whether your experiment comes out exactly like you thought it would. When you're breaking new ground, looking at something no one else has examined or looking at something in a new way, even a negative answer means something. So, no matter how your experiment turns out, the results should leave you with a satisfied sense of accomplishment.

Whatever reason you have for doing a project or designing an experiment doesn't really matter. All that matters is that you get pleasure and satisfaction from your experimental efforts.

Now, let's get to doing something instead of just talking about it!

CHAPTER 2

A Look at Two Science Projects

The first question that may spring to mind is, "Does my science project have to be an experiment?" The answer is an emphatic "no." A science project is any enriching science experience that is not part of your classwork or homework. It is any scientific study, planned and carried out by you. Your project might be related to your school work, but that is not necessary. The format that a science project may take varies. Your science project might be a display of scientific pictures related to some central theme—say, a series of marine fish pictures. It could be a model of the ear that you may have bought and constructed or built from scratch following pictures in an anatomy or biology text. Even a written report on a TV program that presented some new techniques for locating oil beneath the sea qualifies

7

as a science project. However, you may want to do an experiment because it is an exciting learning experience.

Asking the Right Question

A scientific experiment is similar to asking a question. If you ask someone a good question, you will get a satisfactory answer. If your question is vague, the answer will not satisfy you. To illustrate this point, consider this question: "What about your dog?" This is not a good question—it's excessively vague. The answer would have to be another question: "What do you want to know about my dog?" If you had asked, "What color is your dog's fur?" then you would have gotten a specific and definite answer.

So, if you plan and carry out a good experiment, you will get a meaningful result and come to definite conclusions. However, if your experiment is poorly planned and carried out in a sloppy manner, then your results will lead nowhere. For your experiment to be significant, it must follow the scientific method. Your experiment must include:

1. A title containing your hypothesis

2. An experimental design, including an experimental group

3. Collection and recording of data

4. Conclusions based upon the data

The title of your experiment should spell out your **hypothesis**. Your hypothesis is really a possible solution to explain observations or data. It also can act as the reason for predicting new facts. It should be expressed as a statement to be proved or disproved. For example, the hypothesis for an experiment studying the growth of crayfish could be stated as "Small amounts of erythromycin cause red crayfish (*Procambarus clarkii*) to grow more rapidly than normal."

One of the most important things to keep in mind when deciding what experiment to do is that whatever hypothesis you intend to test (prove or disprove), it must not only be explicit (not vague), it must also be one for which the answer can be obtained by objective means; the results must be something you can measure. In other words, this crayfish experiment will be possible because your hypothesis can be tested by data that can be measured—a difference in growth between the crayfish that do receive erythromycin and those that don't. It's not like having an hypothesis that states that erythromycin makes growing red crayfish feel better. You just can't measure that, because you can't ask crayfish how they feel.

Your hypothesis is followed by your plan to discover if erythromycin has any effect upon young crayfish. This is your **experimental design**. In the crayfish experiment, you should plan to set up a number of groups of young crayfish. The more crayfish in each group, the better your results would be. Let's see why. Suppose you had only one crayfish in each group and the crayfish that received the erythromycin died. Then you would conclude that erythromycin caused the crayfish to die. On the other hand, if you had 25 crayfish in each group, and one who had been fed it died but the remainder grew twice the size of the control group, then your results would be far different. All groups must be as similar as possible to each other in all respects, except for one. That one is the group getting the **experimental factor**, which is, in this case, erythromycin. One all-important group is the **control group**. The control represents the normal conditions and is not subjected to any experimental factor.

Let's backtrack for a moment. We said that both the experimental and control groups must be as identical as possible. In both the experimental and control groups you must have the same number of male and female crayfish, of the same size, at the start of the experiment. All groups must receive the same type and amount of food, light and changes of water. Heaters should be provided to keep the water temperature constant for all groups.

One experimental design called for six groups of identical crayfish to be established, with 25 crayfish in each group. So your experimental design would look like this:

> Group I —the control group—no erythromy-
> cin

Group II —addition of 50 mg of erythromycin
with each change of water

Group III—addition of 100 mg of erythromycin
with each change of water

Group IV—addition of 150 mg of erythromycin
with each change of water

Group V —addition of 200 mg of erythromycin
with each change of water

Group VI—addition of 250 mg of erythromycin
with each change of water.

The erythromycin is not only the experimental factor; it is a **variable factor**. We have one control group and *five* experimental groups. As we will see, this is better than establishing only one experimental group.

Your next step is to **collect the data**. Each week, on a particular day, the crayfish in each group will be measured. These figures and the average size for each group would be recorded in a notebook reserved for keeping records of this experiment. If you wished, a coded number could be painted on the back of each crayfish (using a harmless dye or paint). In this way, the increases in growth from week to week could be recorded for individuals within the groups. Let's suppose the experiment was done the easy way—merely recording the average sizes. This data could be summarized in chart form as shown in Table #1. To make the data easier to interpret, it would be wise to make a graph. (See Graph #1).

Table #1 RED CRAYFISH GROWTH
(AVERAGE SIZE IN CM)

Group	Week					
	1	**2**	**3**	**4**	**5**	**6**
I	1.32	2.66	3.78	4.91	5.97	6.8
II	4.38	6.3	7.17	7.38	7.41	7.43
III	2.74	5.14	6.6	7.38	7.6	7.63
IV	4.71	6.74	8.04	8.93	9.48	9.81
V	1.82	3.22	4.37	4.51	4.61	4.63
VI	1.33	1.97	2.44	2.8	2.91	2.92

Your last job is to draw **conclusions** from the data at the end of the experiment. If we only examined the chart, the most striking conclusion is that Group IV, which received 150 mg of erythromycin, grew to the largest size. Other conclusions would be difficult to deduce from the chart. However, let's look at the graph of the same data. We see that more than one conclusion can be arrived at. Some possible conclusions include:

1. 150 mg of erythromycin produced the greatest amount of growth in the shortest time.
2. Concentrations of erythromycin greater than 150 mg (200 mg and 250 mg) stunted the growth of the crayfish. These individuals did not reach the size of those in the control group.
3. In concentrations of 50 mg and 100 mg, only slight increases in length occurred as compared to the size of control group.

A possible application of this project and its results

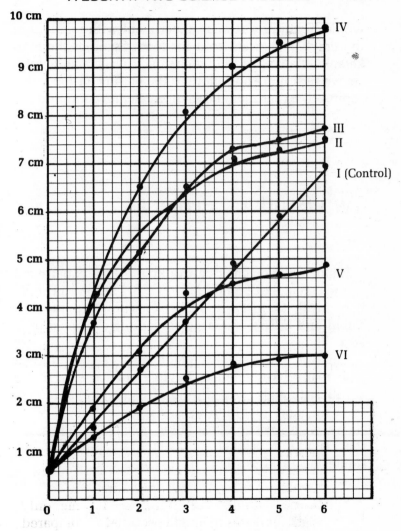

would be to try a similar experiment with relatives of the crayfish that are sold for food. Some of the marketable relatives of the crayfish are lobsters and crabs. As we turn more and more to the oceans for food, this "spin-off" experiment takes on greater meaning and importance.

Two Student Projects

Right now you may be thinking, "That experiment sounds great, but I could never do it." Sure you can do it, or one that is just as good. Let's see how two students, David and Susan, managed to complete science projects.

David is in the seventh grade and is a good student who really likes science. David's not too sure of his abilities, though, and did not feel confident enough to do an experiment for his first science project. When he was eight years old, his father bought him a box kite that David put together and loved to fly. David became interested in kites, their history and how they work. Since he knew something about kites already, David decided to make them the subject of his science project. First, David went to his school library and looked up "kites" in two encyclopedias. What he found was not of too much help, so next he consulted both the card file and the *Reader's Guide To Periodical Literature*. These are both important sources of information for

anyone starting a science project. These sources referred David to:

1. Pelham, David. *The Penguin Book of Kites*. New
   York: Penguin Books, 1976.
2. Yolen, Will. *Kites and Kite Flying*. New York: Simon
   and Schuster, 1976.
3. Streeter, Tal. *The Art of the Japanese Kite*. New
   York: Weatherhill, 1974.
4. *Kite Lines*. Quarterly Journal of the American Kite-
   fliers Association.

David decided that he wanted to prepare a picture
display on the subject of kites. He was able to make
copies of the pictures of many kites, such as a Chinese
Bird Kite and a kite that looked like a cobra. In all, he
had about ten pictures of many kinds of kites. His title
was simply KITES. Placed in several panels near his
most unusual pictures was written information, neatly
printed by David. One panel had as its title FAMOUS
KITE FLYERS. Benjamin Franklin was on the list, as
was Alexander Graham Bell. Even Guglielmo Marconi,
whose radio antenna was held aloft by a large kite, was
mentioned. The other panel was entitled USES OF
KITES. David included holding aerial cameras, as well
as people and radio transmitters, aloft. Another use he
mentioned was recording weather conditions.

In front of the plywood covered with pictures, David
displayed miniature versions of a few unique kite de-
signs. One was a Fighting Kite from East India. Another
was a survival box kite used during World War II.

The judges liked David's display so much that it was
chosen to be shown in his school district's Science Fair.

So you see you don't have to do an experiment to win. Interesting information, well-presented, may be enough to win over your judges.

Susan is older than David. She is an eleventh grader who has already completed a number of science courses. Biology is her favorite and she felt that she wanted to do some kind of experiment with an animal. At first, she had no idea which animal she wanted to work with. Her teacher gave her a few catalogs from biological supply companies. She read one company's brochure on red crayfish. Susan was elated because this seemed like the ideal animal for her to work with. Some of her reasons were that they can be maintained in glass bowls that measure eight to ten inches in diameter and their water need be changed every seven to ten days. Tap water is fine for them, provided it is not acidic. Red crayfish are quite content to eat green plants or even rotten leaves. Normal room temperature is ideal for them and they mature quickly, in six to eight weeks. The female produces 100−400 eggs four to six weeks after mating. Two to three weeks later, the eggs will hatch. For the next couple of weeks, the newborn crayfish attach themselves to their mother. Finally, they become independent. One female could provide Susan with all the crayfish she would need to do the erythromycin experiment that was discussed earlier in this chapter. Yes, Susan's experiment was the one used to illustrate the scientific method.

Let's follow Susan and see how she developed this experiment. She was confident that these aquatic creatures, that grow to a maximum length of only 10 cm, could be easily kept in her home or classroom in glass culture dishes. More important, she was sure that they

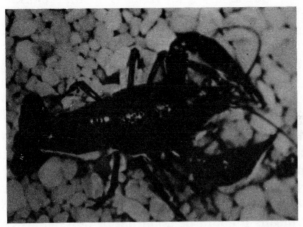

The red crayfish.

would survive and reproduce! Just to be sure, she went to the library and read what she could on crayfish. In addition to the card file and *Reader's Guide*, she also consulted the *Biological Abstracts*. The *Biological Abstracts* are published semi-monthly. Each issue contains abstracts of new information taken from periodicals and journals, published in 90 different countries. By consulting the *Abstracts*, each biological researcher stays up-to-date on what others are doing in his particular area of biology.

Susan soon discovered that not too much had been written on the crayfish in recent years. To be exact, more than twenty years had passed since their reproduction and growth had been investigated. Some of the references that she was able to find were:

1. Penn, G. H., "A Study of the Life History of the Louisiana red crayfish, *Cambarus clarkii* Girard," ECOLOGY, 1943, 24, 1–18

2. Suko, T., "Studies on the Development of the Crayfish." The reproductive cycle, *Science Reports*, VI, 3, 1958, pages 79–91.

Let's take a look at these references and figure out what they're telling us. In reference two, the first information we can glean is that T. Suko is the author of a report entitled "Studies on the Development of the Crayfish." The report centers on the reproductive cycle and the report appeared in a magazine or periodical (that means it could be a journal or newsletter) called *Science Reports* in 1958. The VI after *Science Reports* is the volume number. The "3" that is in front of the date indicates which issue the report appeared in and the final two numbers (79–91) indicate the pages that the report appeared on. Once you've broken down the code that they use in the *Abstracts* and *Reader's Guide*, they can send you right where you need to go to find the information for which you're looking.

At the same time that Susan was doing her readings on the red crayfish, she noticed a newspaper article that mentioned that antibiotics were being fed to cattle, pigs and chickens in order to increase their rate of growth and size at maturity. Susan thought to herself, "What would happen if I fed crayfish antibiotics?" Things happened rapidly after that. She thought of the title for her experiment. It was, "What is the effect of small amounts of erythromycin on the growth of young crayfish (Procambarus clarkii)?"

With her teacher's help, she ordered six crayfish from the biological supply house. They cost less than $10. While she waited for their arrival, she prepared for that eventful day. She collected her culture dishes, gravel and food, and also tested the water from the taps in her home and in the school's chem lab. Fortunately for her, the water was not acidic. The reason Susan selected erythromycin was that a few weeks before, she had a badly infected finger and her doctor had prescribed it. Her recovery was swift and she had about six tablets left over at home. Each tablet contained 250 mg of erythromycin. Using the balances in the chem lab, Susan was able to determine by weight how much of each tablet contained 50 mg of the antibiotic.

At last, the crayfish arrived. She spent the next month handling and observing them as well as learning to care for them properly—in brief, learning all she could about red crayfish by first-hand experience and observation. Soon she was able to pick them up with ease and without fear. She even practiced measuring them with metric rulers. They were like pets and she gave them names.

Finally she was ready. From reading the literature, Susan knew that her crayfish were ready to breed. When the young left their mother and began an independent life, she divided them into six groups of 25 crayfish per group. This meant a lot of bowls for Susan to care for and clean, but she managed. Each group was kept in marked bowls. Susan tried to keep all the living conditions identical for each group. The only difference was the measured amounts of erythromycin added to the water weekly. Naturally, the control group did not receive any of the antibiotic.

Every Saturday morning, for six consecutive weeks, Susan measured the length of each crayfish in centimeters. The measurements for each group were recorded, as well as the weekly averages. If a crayfish in one of the groups died, the remaining crayfish would be used to determine the average length for that group. Graph 1 and Table 1 present the data that Susan collected.

In addition to her written report, Susan displayed some color photographs of her crayfish. Enlarged pictures of her table and graph and the photographs were artistically arranged on several pieces of heavy cardboard. Her display was completed by the addition of three bowls of living crayfish for the judges and the public to view at the Science Fair.

If David and Susan can complete winning projects, you can too... with a little help!

Interviews with Science Winners

This is Cherise Dyal (16 years old) shortly after she became a semi-finalist in the 1981 Westinghouse Science Talent Search. The title of her winning project was, "Genetic Observation on Mutant *Heliconius cydno.*" Perhaps her experiences and advice can be of help to you.

Question: What is *Heliconius cydno?*
Answer: Oh, that is a species of butterfly.
Question: How long did you work on this project?
Answer: Two months.
Question: How did you happen to select this partic-
           ular project?
Answer: I participated in a National Science Foun-
           dation Summer Program at Austin, Texas
           last summer. They presented me with the
           butterflies and told me to do whatever I
           liked with them. The obvious thing at the
           time seemed to be to try and figure out the
           genetics of this butterfly since it was a mu-
           tant.

Question: How did you feel when they said, "Do something with it!"

Answer: LOST! I didn't know where to begin. So I figured I would start rearing eggs and breeding them, trying to get as many as I could.

Question: Who worked with you?

Answer: I was the only student in the program using them. There was a graduate student there who was supposed to give me some guidance on it. He did help me out but I did most of it myself.

Question: Did you use the library very much for this project?

Answer: I used the library to help me find the best techniques for culturing them. I also used the library to read up on the principles of mimicry. This is what I thought might be involved at first.

Question: Which part of the project did you find to be the most difficult?

Answer: Analyzing the data after collecting a large amount of it. The next thing was to see what I had. So the hardest part was thinking of some hypothesis to investigate and then coming up with answers. For that, I got some help from the scientist who helped me develop some of my ideas.

Question: What sort of scientific tools did you use to investigate the genetics?

Answer: Another student in the NSF Summer Program was working with the electron microscope. So I gave him some specimens and had him analyze them. What the structure looked like. That is, the patch of white or yellow or both.

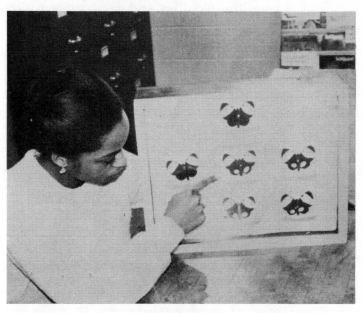

Question: Approximately how many butterflies did
            you work with?
Answer: About 120 or so. But many more eggs. The
            120 were those that I successfully raised
            from eggs.
Question: How did you feel when you learned that
            you were one of 300 in the entire country
            who were in the Westinghouse Honors
            Group?
Answer: I was very happy and excited.
Question: What advice would you give someone who
            is just starting a science project?

Answer: The first thing is that it is a lot easier if you are in a Summer NSF program because they have the facilities and you can work on your project every day. In school, I found that I could only spare time one or two days a week when I was doing my earlier projects. The second thing is to really understand the organism you are working with before you start. If you don't, you may find that you don't like the organism and this makes your project difficult. You should really research your organism before starting—go to the library and read up, talk with whatever experts you can get to.

Smiling at you from the left is 16 year old Scott Lepson. On the right is Sal Gabino, who is a year younger. For the last three years, they have combined their efforts on a number of different solar energy projects. The title of their latest project is "Can a Heat Pipe Increase the Efficiency of a Flat Plate Solar Collector?"

Question: What is a heat pipe?

Sal: It is a pipe that has been vacuumized [holds a slight vacuum] and has a small amount of fluid in it. The heat pipe connects the solar collector to the place where the heat is stored.

Question: How long have you worked on this project?

Scott: We started our initial research last summer. Our construction started in December [this interview took place early in April]. But we have been researching solar energy for the past two or three years.

Question: Why did you pick solar energy?

Sal: I was looking for a science project in the ninth grade and came across a flat plate collector of solar energy in a World Encyclopedia.

Question: Why were you looking for a science project?

Scott: Our science teacher gave us the inspiration to do one.

Question: How did you two form a partnership?

Scott: We kind of approached one another, and Sal's idea of building a regular flat plate solar collector looked appealing. So, I asked him if we could do this together. We did do it together and placed third in the Science Fair that year.

Question: What other awards have you won from then to now?

Sal: The next year we built a hydro-anima collector. This collector won in both the local Fair and in SEER. In SEER, we won a couple of corporate awards. One award was a luncheon at the company plant. Another was a trip to see the company's plants in operation. We won a tour of the World Trade Center from the Port Authority of New York.

Question: What are you two planning to enter this year?

Scott: We already placed second in the Borough Fair and we plan to enter SEER again this year.

Question: What do you look forward to in your senior year?

Sal: We look forward to Westinghouse. But Westinghouse won't accept a group project, so we are now starting to separate the project into two distinct parts.

Question: Who helped you with your projects?

Scott: Teachers and parents. We wrote many letters to obtain information. The letters went to universities like Brooklyn Polytech. We also wrote to solar energy companies and to the Battelle Institute in Columbus, Ohio. They developed the heat pipe for *passive* solar applications. Ours is for *active* solar applications.

Question: Did you use the library to any great extent?

Sal: We used the microfilm of the *New York Times Index* a lot.

Scott: Last summer, I used the library extensively looking for books on applications of solar energy.

Question: How did you feel after winning the Borough Fair and SEER last year?

Sal: Exhilarating! You can't put that great feeling into words.

Question: What advice would you give someone just starting a science project?

Sal: Pick a field that interests you but isn't out of reach like high energy nuclear physics.

Scott: Another point is when you actually start out and you have a topic in mind, try to find teachers who are in your field and ask their advice. Make use of their experience. In the ninth grade, we talked to one of the teachers who had solar panels on his house. He built them himself and was able to give us a lot of guidance.

Question: Is there anything you would like to say to our readers?

Sal: You have to do your own research. You can't ask someone, "What is solar energy?" We started researching in the beginning and we have been doing it ever since.

Scott: It is not an overnight thing to develop a science project. It takes more than a week, a month—at least a couple of months and extensive research.

CHAPTER 3

Literary Sources

Let's assume that you have selected a suitable topic and are fairly certain about what you want to do. Now, you may not be too sure how to carry out your investigation, collect data properly or draw valid conclusions. Don't worry—here's a guide for the path to success.

No matter what your project may be, your first move is to *go to the library!* Whatever field of science you have decided upon, you can be reasonably sure that some research has already been done. Other investigators have done some of the groundwork for you. Their work, methods and results have been recorded somewhere and all you have to do is find it and use it to help you with your science project. Reading what others have done will have a bearing upon how you will conduct your own scientific venture.

A Sample Project

Let's say that organic polymers that conduct electricity is your topic. A young student might want to do a report—either verbal or visual—on this relatively new field. A graduating senior might be intrigued with the thought of discovering a stable polymer that would conduct electricity. This is also the goal of a number of research chemists.

Regardless of the nature of his or her project, both students would start their work on polymers in their school library. Here, they would spend hours searching out the articles and books on this topic. This takes time and patience.

When they get to the library, the *card file* should be their first stop. This file lists all the books on the shelves in three ways—according to title, author and subject. The cards are all arranged alphabetically. The trend in libraries has been toward creating a separate subject card file with author and title in separate files. Another trend is for putting all the information that is in the card file into a computer.

The first headings that the youngsters should look at are: chemistry, organic chemistry, polymers and electricity. When deciding which books to examine, look at the dates of publication. The date may give you an idea how relevant the information is. If you were doing a report on the history of polymers, a book written ten or fifteen years ago could not be very useful. Remember, in some cases a book published last year may now be out of date due to some very recent discovery.

Ask the librarian to show you the *vertical file*, particularly if you are doing a written or pictorial report. The vertical file contains current booklets and pamphlets that the library has received, arranged by subjects. You may be pleasantly surprised to discover a very informative and useful source in the vertical file. Next, you should read the same topics in an encyclopedia of science and technology. Some encyclopedias contain technical information while others merely give the reader an idea of the important concepts.

The Monthly Mine

Let's leave the books in the library and look at the magazines and journals. As its title indicates, you should consult the *Reader's Guide to Periodical Literature*. A soft-covered edition is published every two months, in addition to a yearly hard-covered edition. The *Guide* is arranged by topics. A short synopsis of each article is included, as well as the name of the publication, the particular volume and the pages where it can be found.

For science projects, don't overlook the value of *The New York Times*, especially since they have started publishing a special weekly science section. Consult their index, which, like most indexes, will tell you in

The Reader's Guide to Periodical Literature is made up of many volumes.

capsule form about the various stories or articles. It tells you the date and page on which you can find it and even in which column the news item appears. Given a brief idea of the contents, you can quickly decide whether it is worthwhile to read the entire article. You don't even have to handle the newspaper since if it is more than a few weeks old it will be on microfilm.

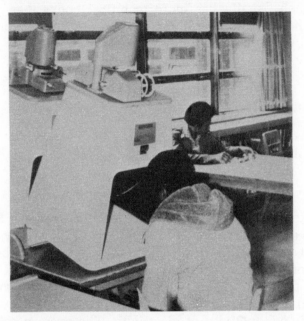

Reading *The New York Times* on microfilm.

Other important indexes that you should look over in your search of the literature are those of *Science* and *Scientific American*. Both of these excellent publications have their articles indexed in the periodical guide mentioned earlier, but you will find more comprehensive summaries of the articles in the magazines' indexes.

Your next stop in your literary search should be the main branch of your local library system. If that is not possible, then a visit to your local branch will have to do. Again, check the card file first. The library's main branch usually has more technical books than your school library. Your library system services both adults and young people, while the school library deals with only school-age youngsters.

The Textbook Trail

Recent college textbooks are excellent sources. Read the chapters that deal with your topic. You may find that you will have to look in five or more textbooks before you have gathered sufficient information. Using the polymer project as an example, you would have to read about polymers, the cause of their instability and their conductivity of electricity. The average college textbook would just give you a fine overview of these topics.

Where do you find college textbooks and how do you find the topic you're looking for? A visit to a college bookstore is one possibility. College bookstores have copies of all the textbooks that the professors are using in their courses. These will be the latest, best sources of information possible. Checking the textbooks for organic chemistry, electrical engineering or other relevant topics will enable you to find which books are worth further examination. Your further examination should consist of taking a look at the book's index or table of contents and seeing if there is any reference to your subject. If there is, you can then proceed to the university library. There, you may find that there are copies of textbooks for all the courses being taught, including the books you've just found at the bookstore.

At the end of each chapter in most college textbooks you will find a list of references that the author used for writing that particular chapter. You can backtrack and read his original sources. This often pays off in unexpected ways, because the writer of the textbook may ignore an important point made by the investigator in the original source. It is also possible that the author of the textbook has misquoted the original scientist.

The *Subject Guide to Books in Print* is a wonderful library tool. Like the card catalog, the *Subject Guide* (from R. R. Bowker) lists books by their topic and this makes it very easy for any researcher to zero in on one topic of interest. And, since the subject guides come out annually, you can concentrate on the very latest information. Unfortunately, the *Guide* lists only the title, author, publisher, cost and year of publication—there is no summary and that means you'll probably have to look at the book. But, you'll find searching the shelves a fascinating process.

The *Subject Guide* may steer you to highly specialized textbooks with titles such as *Electromagnetic Scattering* or *Polymer Blends*. Books of this type may not be too helpful. They may not have the information that you need, or they may be so highly technical that you can't understand what you are reading. You could read a highly technical book or article if you have a dictionary of scientific terms close by for reference purposes. It is not uncommon for high school students to read a technical paper or book three or four times before it makes sense to them.

Reading Research

You can also read other research articles on your topic. These are in technical journals. Usually the title of the journal gives you a clue as to the kind of articles it will contain. It is fairly obvious what kind of articles you will find in the *Journal of the American Chemical Society*. Often, you can narrow down your search by using guides and indexes. We have already mentioned a few, including the *Reader's Guide To Periodical Literature*. An even better source for the scientist's purposes is to consult the *Science Citation Index*. This is better than the *Reader's Guide* because it is cumulative, meaning that new articles on a particular subject are added to those of past years. The *Science Citation Index* deals only with scientific topics and is more specialized than the *Reader's Guide*.

Each branch of science has its own special language that is often meaningless to all except researchers in that particular field. Do you know in which branch of science the following terms are used—restriction endonucleases, ligase, chimeric plasmids, lambda vehicles and charon phage? If you said the field of recombinant DNA (or genetic engineering), you were correct. Other big problems are that the concepts are difficult to understand or they are expressed in complicated chemical and mathematical formulas. One of the reasons why it's suggested that you read a college text or two is because they will define the terms and formulas that the writer of research articles assumes the reader already knows.

Scientific papers appear in standardized form. An *abstract* usually follows the title. A brief *introduction* comes next, then the *experimental design* will be outlined. The abstract is simply a summary and may be all you need to read. The *data* follows with a discussion and interpretation and, finally, the *conclusions*. The author's *name* and *address* are indicated, and finally his *references* and *notes*.

The best source of scientific journals is *Ayer's Dictionary of Publications*. This directory is published yearly and updates all the periodicals and journals printed in the United States. The entries are arranged in several ways, including by subject. If you want to know what scientists in other countries are doing, consult *Ulrich's International Periodical Directory*. You can be reasonably sure that only university and college libraries would have the journals listed in *Ulrich's*.

If you find that reading professional journals is beyond your ability, then you should turn to the *Abstracts*. If your local library can't get them, you can be almost certain to find them in most college libraries. *Abstracts* are special journals that feature short reviews of key articles that appear in other journals. They can help you understand some of the complicated articles that you have already read but did not fully understand.

They also could help you decide which technical articles you should read *thoroughly*. There are many abstracts, almost as many as there are special branches of science; for example, *Chemical Abstracts* or *Physical Abstracts*.

As useful as abstracts are magazines that feature review articles. *Bacteriological Reviews* is just one example. Here, articles will give you an overview of all the work done in a particular scientific area. If you were interested in the topic of radioactivity, the review article would start with the work of Becquerel (one of the pioneers in the field) and proceed to the most recent advances. Most review articles include an extensive list of references, some of which, if read in their entirety, could prove to be useful to you. The *Applied Mechanics Review* is another useful publication that specializes in articles and books on mechanical engineering. Both *Science* and *Scientific American* publish review articles from time to time.

Take Note! Make Notes!

Reading an article or a chapter in a reference volume takes time, but you are not finished after you have completed your reading. That's right! You better make a record of what you have just read. Right now it is fresh in your mind, but how much will you recall a month from now? Write it down and then it doesn't matter if you forget the details.

Develop a system for taking notes. Don't use any handy scrap of paper, such as a candy wrapper! If you do, you will soon have a drawer full of scraps of paper and sorting them out into a meaningful order will take as much time as your original research. Some students use a special notebook to record their readings, but I prefer a card system, using 3- by 5-inch index cards. It is easy to sort and arrange them in any order you want. At the top of the index card, print the *title* of the article or of the book. Indicate the *date of publication*, the *author's name* and the specific *pages you read*. If your reference is a periodical such as *Science*, enter the *date, volume* and *number*—for example, "'Experiments in Sensory Deprivation,' *Science*, April 13, 1979, Vol. 204, No. 4389." Each index card should be headed in the same way. Use the rest of the card for recording what you have learned that pertains to your science project.

Since your notes are so important, take care not to lose them or else you will have to search your sources out again. Your notes on the index cards have a number of uses. First of all, they give you a summary of the work that has been done in the field you are investigating. They also bring you up-to-date and give you a brief history of the scientific studies done in this branch of science. They have importance when you are giving an oral presentation at a scientific competition. It is very impressive to say to the judges, "The concept of allometric space as described by Oster and Wilson in their book, *Caste and Ecology in the Social Insects*, has a number of implications for 'niche width' of ants. I have investigated two of them." By referring to your index cards before being interviewed, you can easily recall the book, authors and the important information.

Write On

You may feel the urge to write to the author of a research paper because you believe that you need the help of a professional in order to plan your experiment properly. Follow that urge if you want to locate detailed information after reading an abstract that briefly summarized a research article. Another case that calls for writing is if you have read someone's paper and some point in it is not clear or was not mentioned. In both of these cases, you can be reasonably sure of getting a response from the scientist. Let's take two specific cases and see how best to word your letters of inquiry so that you will get a response.

Let's imagine you decided to experiment with producing mutations in *Clostridium acetobutylicum* in the hopes of producing a high yield of butanol. Butanol's properties are very similar to diesel fuel and gasoline. It can be produced by the fermentation of potatoes by the anaerobic *Clostridium* bacteria. You had read that Professor Antonio Moreira of Colorado State University was conducting experiments using the whey of milk as blending agent and is trying to increase the extremely low yield (1.2%) of butanol per fermentation batch. Since you read an announcement of Dr. Moreira's work in an issue of *Science News* (Vol. 117, No. 15, 4/12/80) which gave no details, you had no idea of the specifics of his work. It would not do to write him and say, "Please design an experiment I can do to try and increase the yield of butanol by *Clostridium acetobutylicum* fermenting potatoes. Kindly send this by return mail as I want to get started as soon as possible!" It is extremely doubtful that he would reply. It is better if your letter asks where you can find his paper on this topic and also any other references that he feels you should read. And from these you may be able to put together an experiment of your own. If, after you read his article in detail and something was either unclear or missing—for example, if he failed to mention the temperature at which the fermentation took place— then you should write asking for details as in the following model letter.

Request for original research paper

Dr. Antonio Moreira
Colorado State University
Fort Collins, Colorado 80521

Dear Dr. Moreira,

I am currently planning to experiment on improving the yield of butanol by using mutant forms of *Clostridium acetobutylicum*. I hope that one of the mutant forms will produce a high yield of butanol. I read a brief digest of your work on butanol in an issue of *Science News*. Please tell me where your original paper is published or kindly send me a copy. If you have a list of other references that you feel I should read, please send them also, if it is not too much trouble. Your help will be deeply appreciated.

Sincerely,

Request for additional information

Dr. Antonio Moreira
Colorado State University
Fort Collins, Colorado 80521

Dear Dr. Moreira,

I recently read your paper on acetone-butanol fermentation. Since I am planning to do a related experiment using mutated forms *Clostridium acetobutylicum* fermenting potatoes, I would like to know at what temperature did you find the yield of butanol to be the highest? I could not find that information in your article.

Sincerely,

These letters are proper requests for information. Don't just write to the first scientist you get an address for, hoping that he or she will put together a prize-winning experiment for you.

For Example

In a recent Science Fair, one entrant's project involved determining whether house crickets possess internal biological clocks. You might do a similar experiment using insects around your house. For example, whether the aphids that feed on your garden plants have a biological rhythm and can it be used against them—is there a time of day or a period in the rhythm during which they are weaker or when likeliest to die if exposed to insecticides? Such a project could have important implications, since aphids are harmful insects that suck out the juices of plants.

Another Science Fair winner investigated the packing density and burn efficiency of rocket fuel. You might decide to investigate the burn efficiency of gasohol as compared with both gasoline and alcohol. (This is one of those somewhat hazardous projects that should only be undertaken with adult supervision.)

In a recent Student Exposition on Energy Resources (SEER), one of the top winners' project dealt with the harnessing of wave power. You might have a design for improving the efficiency of wind power conversion to electricity.

The point here is that very few science projects are unique. This is true not only for the young scientist but for the adult professional as well. Almost all scientific achievements have been based upon the work of others.

Just consider that the manufacture of vaccines for use against virus diseases, such as measles, was dependent upon the ability to grow the viruses in flasks in order to carry on the necessary research. As a result, it was impossible for any scientist to perfect a vaccine against a virus disease until an earlier scientist had perfected a technique for growing viruses in glass tubes. Normally, viruses only reproduce inside of living cells.

Likewise, we could never have placed a man on the moon in 1900! Think of all the scientific breakthroughs and technological advances that were made since 1900 in order for us to put a man on the moon in 1969.

So, don't be afraid to use someone else's project or findings as a starting place for your scientific endeavor. In fact, looking at the winners and the also-rans from last year's Fair might be an excellent place to start your research. There, you'll find projects and processes that you can go one step beyond and maybe just win it all.

CHAPTER 4

Now, You're Ready to Do a Science Project!

What kind of science project would you like to do? Are you good with tools, or is soldering electrical circuits fun to you? Perhaps, best of all, you love to read! No matter what your likes and dislikes are, there is a science project for you. In this chapter, let's consider some types of projects that are appropriate for elementary and secondary school students.

Pictorial Display

One of the easiest and most enjoyable science projects is making a *Pictorial Display*. Displays can explore recent scientific developments—for example, a display entitled "Recent Developments in Re-Attaching Amputated Limbs" could use photos, drawings and diagrams to explain this successful new medical technique. Or, pictures can be used to relate the history of a scientific device. The development of the airplane could consist of a display of pictures of airplanes beginning with the Wright Brothers' first plane and continuing on to the supersonic fighters and transports of today.

When designing your display, there are a few simple tips that may make a good display *great*. Mounted on oaktag or cardboard covered with construction paper, a display can be made attractive with little effort. Be sure your title will catch the viewer's eye. Include a few printed comments or explanations along with the pictures. Good sources of pictures are newspapers, magazines, pamphlets and booklets printed by government agencies or business concerns. Almost any large corporation like the Ford Motor Company, General Motors or General Foods will supply you with all sorts of pictures. Your local gas and electric company will send you pictures and pamphlets relating to energy, including alternative energy sources such as solar and geothermal energy. (Chapter 10 will list these sources and many others.)

Observations must be made periodically and with care.

Suppose you decide to prepare a picture display entitled, "The Scientific Discoveries of Voyager II." For this you would use pictures, photographs, maps, charts and diagrams from NASA (National Aeronautic and Space Administration) and NASA publications. You would include, possibly, photographs from the magazine section of your local newspaper or from a recent issue of a magazine such as *Life* that specializes in picture coverage of various events. If you can't remove the pictures from a publication, it is always possible to use a copying machine to make a copy that you can do with what you please. Most libraries and many stores have these machines available for your use at a small cost per copy.

Another pictorial project might be entitled, "New Methods of Repairing Damaged Arteries and Veins." If you like this topic, it would be worthwhile to ask your family doctor if he could give you some medical journals with pictures and articles on it. (In fact, your family doctor is a good source of topics. Mention to him that you're working on a science project.) Don't be afraid to ask people you know for material. You will find that local business people and family friends will be more than happy to provide you with sources of pictures for your project if they can.

The key ingredients for a successful pictorial display done by a young science student are large, colorful pictures that are artistically arranged. You will need a carefully printed title that will call attention to your display, and a short written summary that explains the point you are trying to make. Be sure your summary mentions why your display is important. For example, if you do a display about weather forecasting, mention how important it is to farmers, pilots and businessmen.

Many teachers like this kind of science project because they make useful learning displays for bulletin boards in classrooms and in halls. In turn, your project may spark someone else to become curious and interested enough to do a science project similar to yours.

Some people collect stamps or coins while others collect items that can be used to make a science project. Leaves from the trees in your neighborhood can be collected, pressed flat, and used to explain the local eco-

Colorful, neat titles and labels are an asset to any report or display.

system. Or, they can simply be arranged on colored construction paper with the title "Leaves from Trees Around My House." It would be wise to print the name of the tree under or next to each different leaf. Add to this a short statement about each tree and you have a decorative and informative display. Seashells, rocks or butterflies are other possible collections that can be converted into a science display.

It has been said that a picture is worth a thousand words. It's not always true. There are some topics that you just can't do justice to with pictures. For example, it would be hard to put together a pictorial display about the effect of noise pollution on hearing that would work a tenth as well as a very simple written report.

Actually, there are more *written reports* turned in as science projects than anything else. Now, there is a tendency among some students to copy a section from an encyclopedia or other reference work word for word and then submit that for their extra credits. And, other students sometimes "summarize" the main ideas from several books or other sources—that means they take chunks of copy, word for word, from several places instead of just one—and turn that in as a project. *Sometimes* these techniques work; more often, the teacher manages to recognize the fact that this just isn't written in the student's usual style and somebody gets embarrassed instead of getting extra credit. So, do it yourself—use sources but put their information into your own words.

There are many, many sources of information for written reports. They include library reference books, newspaper articles and stories, magazines of all sorts, encyclopedias, booklets and pamphlets from scientific organizations such as the AAAS (The American Association for the Advancement of Science). Still other sources are government agencies and industrial corporations.

It is always helpful to include pictures, charts or graphs in order to make your written report more informative and interesting. Pictures would be an asset to a report on "Making Gasohol From Garbage" or "Drilling for Oil Beneath the Sea." Pictures really will help. Also, try to add a touch of originality at the end of the report by providing some thoughts of your own. For example, has much progress been made in this field so far? Why are the ideas presented important and useful? What problems of a scientific, social or political nature may result from what you have written about?

A written report need not be done only on written material. Television specials, such as the PBS program "The Workings of the Mind," could serve as the basis for a written report. Be sure to read the description of the program in your newspaper or in *TV Guide* and check to see if there have been any articles written about the program. This will prepare you for viewing. Then, take notes while you watch. You might decide to combine your learnings from the TV program with information gained from books. Compare what you learn from the books with what the TV program showed you. For example, the TV program may have some recent information which as yet has not been published.

Certain motion pictures lend themselves to being the subject of a written science report. *The China Syndrome* was a popular motion picture that dealt with a possible dangerous accident at a nuclear power plant. It certainly could have been the subject of a science report. For example, a comparison of the movie accident with the reports on the real accident at Three Mile Island could be very informative.

When doing a report on a motion picture, it might

be wise to include some advertisements for the film cut out from your local newspaper. Be sure to read what the movie critics say about the film. Read, too, what the science writers in the newspapers write about the film. Sometimes the motion picture may have scientific errors that would detract from your report if they were included—or you could even do a report on the scientific errors and why or how they were made.

Models

Models are a favorite project format for many young science students. Models are often seen at Science Fairs. They can be made of clay, plastic, cardboard, plaster of paris, paper mache, wood or metal. Similar to clothes, some models become fashionable for awhile,

An entry in the Brookhaven National Laboratory's Model Bridge Contest.

then go out of style. Models of nuclear energy plants were seen in great numbers after the Three Mile Island accident. And models of volcanos, complete with fire and "erupting lava," are seen year after year.

Rather than making models using the materials already mentioned, some young people prefer to buy a factory-made model. In this category are miniature replicas of prehistoric animals, model jet planes and engines, as well as plastic skeletons and parts of the human body such as the eye and ear.

Most judges and teachers prefer models that are made

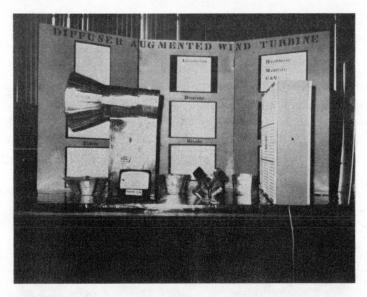

The builder of this wind turbine included a fan and a meter to prove that the turbine really works.

by students rather than a store-bought kit that was assembled. Obviously much more work and effort goes into the making of a model of a dam or a hydroelectric generator out of wood and metal than a precise model of an ear that was bought in a department store.

Flashing lights, moving gears and whirling propeller blades are much more exciting and usually get much more attention than a stationary cut-away model of an automobile engine. It makes sense that if a model is good, then a working model or one with moving parts must be better. This is often the thinking of students in search of a project. Some working models are easy to construct. Electric motors and transformers can be made with wire, an iron nail, metal from a food can and a few magnets. Some students take the easy way out. Instead of making a working model from inexpensive basic parts, they buy a kit of electronic components and assemble the kit into one of many possible electronic gadgets. It is possible to buy a kit and build an AM radio or a burglar alarm system that will sound a siren when a light beam is interrupted. Kits of this type are available at stores such as Radio Shack. You can make a strobe light, an electric bell circuit or a series of lights that will go on and off in a random pattern. Perhaps you would like to build a metal detector and search for coins at a nearby beach or picnic area after the detector has served its purpose as a scientific project.

Energy-saving devices such as solar cells can produce small but useful amounts of electric current, enough current to power a small radio. These are available from many electronic supply houses. Windmills and hydroelectric turbines also fall into the category of energy-saving devices that you can construct as science projects.

The main idea behind assembling a working model should not be to prove that you can follow instructions, such as, "fasten part A to part B using three ½-inch bolts." Rather, your working model should demonstrate a technological advance or a scientific principle much in the news, like energy.

When your working model is finished, add a title and labels as well as a brief written summary on the scientific concepts behind your model or the scientific progress it illustrates. For example, the electric dynamo demonstrates that, by moving a magnet in and out of a coil of wire, an electric current will be produced. Another easy and popular working model you can make is the electromagnet. All you need is a coil of wire, an iron nail and a dry cell. You could also use a C or D flashlight battery. With these materials, you can show that the strength of the electromagnet will vary with the size of the coil, the core (iron nail) or the amount of current.

Remember that it is more to your advantage to build a simple working model from common materials than to assemble a complicated kit such as a prewired CB radio transceiver or a two-station intercom set-up.

More and more, as computers become part of our lives, so too will their popularity as a science project increase. Mini-computers are seen in increasing numbers at Science Fairs and are often submitted as science projects. They, too, can be bought at many electronics supply stores in kit form.

Living Models

Have you considered building an ecosystem—making a working model of a woodland forest or a tropical lake? This is what you are really doing when you establish a terrarium or an aquarium. These living and working models are excellent beginning projects for anyone, especially younger students. Sometimes they develop into life-long hobbies that provide years of pleasure and enjoyment.

The simplest terrarium to make and care for is the desert terrarium. All that is necessary are a few cacti and some cactus planting mix. An old aquarium makes an ideal container for this project. The addition of several rocks will add to the beauty of your miniature desert. Avoid using any desert animals such as lizards unless you are willing to care for them. Since desert plants thrive on "careful neglect" (they need water about once a month), they are ideal for anyone who would have difficulty following a precise watering schedule.

Repeating a Classic Experiment

Some people prefer to repeat a famous scientist's experiment as their project. There is nothing wrong with this; replication is an important part of the scientific process. Every experimenter must share his procedure with all other scientists and for an experiment to be believed, the results should be the same as those found by the originator of the experiment no matter who repeats it. Repeating a classic experiment is a good way of getting the "feel" of doing a scientific experiment.

If the field of genetics is of interest to you, why not repeat some of Gregor Mendel's experiments? In one case, he crossed a large number of pure tall pea plants with short pea plants. All you need for this experiment are the correct sweet pea seeds and a garden in which to grow them.

Or, you could repeat the experiments of Alexander Fleming, the discoverer of penicillin, or even the work of Louis Pasteur, who definitely disproved the belief that bacteria arise from the air by the process of spontaneous generation. This was not easy for Pasteur to do in the year of 1862. However, now you can follow his procedures with ease. I recommend the book entitled *Great Experiments in Biology*, by Gabriel Fogel, if you are interested in repeating classic biological experiments.

Perhaps your interests lie in chemistry or physics rather than in biology. If so, there are a vast number of landmark experiments that you may re-do for a science project.

Alessandro Volta designed the electrophorus (a device for producing electrical charges). The materials you need to duplicate his experiment are relatively simple to obtain. You will need a piece of wool, an old phonograph record and an aluminum pie plate to which you have attached a 20-centimeter length of nylon thread or cord. A drop of rubber cement works well for attaching the nylon to the pie plate's center. The electrophorus works best when the air is dry, so don't try this on a humid August day. Rub the record with the piece of wool for approximately a half a minute. Then, using the nylon cord or thread as a handle, place the pie plate on top of the record. If you now touch the pie plate with your finger, you will feel a slight shock and see a small spark. The explanation is based upon the fact that all matter is made up of electrical charges. The reason we normally are not shocked when we touch something is that the number of positive and negative charges are equal (see Fig. 1). During the rubbing some of the electrons, the negatively charged particles in the atoms of the wool, move onto the phonograph record. This means that the record is negatively charged (Fig. 2). When the pie plate is placed on top of the phonograph record, the plate's positive charges are attracted to the many negative charges in the record upon which the pie plate is resting. The negative charges in the pie plate are repelled by the record's negativity and they move as far away from the phonograph record as they can (Fig. 3). Your finger provides an escape route for the electrons on the pie plate. When your finger comes close to the top of the pie plate, the electrons jump from the plate to your finger even before you touch the plate. This causes the spark and the tiny shock. The electrons go through your body into the ground (Fig. 4). The construction of the electrophorus can be the starting place for a report on some experiments with static electricity.

If chemistry is what you're interested in, then per-

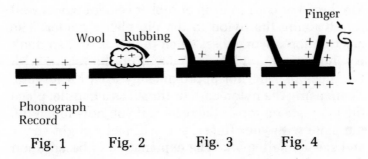

Fig. 1   Fig. 2   Fig. 3   Fig. 4

haps you'd like to make some oxygen. Joseph Priestley, who has been called "The Father of Chemistry," discovered oxygen on August 1, 1774. He used a glass lens to concentrate the sun's rays and thus heat a small amount of mercuric oxide in a closed bottle. The mercuric oxide decomposed into a colorless gas and the metal mercury. The colorless gas was oxygen. This is one famous experiment that you should NOT repeat unless you modify it somewhat, for safety's sake. Mercury is a poisonous metal that can be absorbed through the skin of your fingers if you touch it. Instead of mercuric oxide, substitute potassium chlorate, which will decompose into potassium chloride and oxygen. Potassium chloride is not a poison. This reaction will work better if another safe chemical, manganese dioxide, is added as a catalyst. Your teacher can help you obtain these two safe, simple chemicals.

The list of outstanding experiments is quite long and would more than fill this entire book. If this type of science project appeals to you, select and read textbooks and references in your area of interest. You will find many classic experiments described in these books. Pick one that you can do. Keep in mind what equipment and materials you will need. Can you get them easily? Most important of all is the question of safety. Don't attempt anything that might result in you being burned, cut, poisoned or shocked by electricity. You don't want a fire or explosion to occur in your home. Before attempting any experiment, consult your science teacher and your parents to be absolutely sure that what you want to do is safe and appropriate for you.

Without question, the most difficult type of science project to attempt is the design and completion of an original science experiment. Much more will be said about experiments in the next chapter of this book. For the time being, let us consider only a few sources of inspiration for a scientific experiment. What you are studying in school can often be your best source of ideas. If you are studying magnets, you might decide to investigate the strengths of magnetic fields of force around magnets of different shapes (bar, horseshoe, circular, etc.) Or if you are studying surface tension, you might feel that an investigation of the effect of detergents upon the surface tension of water would be a fascinating experiment for you to do.

Store-Bought Experiments

Looking through the catalog of a scientific supply house, such as Edmund Scientific Company, can raise

A good science project often includes a novel invention.

questions in your mind that can lead to an experiment. For example, in the *Schoolmasters' Science and Teaching Aids Catalog* is an ad for a water and nutrient solution for growing plants. The ad states, "Plants grow up to 10 times faster...." You might decide to grow plants in their special solution and in garden soil to determine scientifically the accuracy of that statement. Or you might be intrigued by something you read in the newspapers or in a scientific magazine. An issue of *The Sciences*, published by The New York Academy of Sciences, carried the story of Elso Barhoorn, who made artificial fossils of algae using a method called "silicification." You could write to him and ask where you might read details of his method. If you are able to duplicate his procedures, you might devise the following experiment: "How Do Artificial Fossils Compare To Natural Ones?"

Don't attempt to carry out an original scientific experiment unless you have a sincere desire to do *all* the work involved. As you will see later on in this book, many problems and frustrations can arise while experimenting. If you are not dedicated to your experiment or if you have trouble handling frustrations, then it would be better to select another type of science project. On the other hand, if the challenge of an investigation appeals to you, be sure to read Chapters 5 through 10 with care.

Surveys

Another impressive type of science project is the scientific survey. An example of a simple survey would be to discover how many different species of trees and the number of each species growing in a quarter-mile-square area of your house. Sometimes the results of a survey are unexpected and surprising. In writing up the tree survey mentioned earlier, it would be helpful to include a table listing first the species of tree with the largest number of individuals, and so on. The last entry on the table would be the species with the fewest individuals. This data could be nicely displayed in graph form as well. Pictures of some of the trees included in the final report would add color and embellish the report of your survey.

Don't think that you must live in the country to do a survey. There are many surveys that anyone can do. For example, you might survey the students in your class or grade and find out how many do not eat breakfast. This information could then be correlated to the number of absences for each student over a three month period. Thus, you might determine that those who don't eat breakfast have a significantly higher absence rate than those who do eat breakfast. Surveys are very useful for determining if there is a relationship between seemingly unrelated sets of data, as this survey dealing with eating of breakfast and rate of absence clearly shows.

For some surveys, it is not even necessary for you to get the data yourself. You can use statistics compiled by others. Suppose you were interested in relating cigarette smoking for the past 25 years to the number of deaths from strokes (cerebral accidents). You would get your data from government sources, medical sources and the tobacco industry. It would be best to plot the number of cigarettes smoked year by year on a graph. On the same graph, you could plot the number of deaths from strokes. The information should also be displayed in a table or chart form with these headings: YEAR/NUMBER OF CIGARETTES SMOKED/NUMBER OF DEATHS FROM STROKES. Both sets of data may have been available to everyone but you might be the first to determine the scientific relationship between the two. In fact, you might just compare the claims of the tobacco industry with those of the Surgeon General.

The range of surveys that can be done is very broad as well as being interesting and informative. Would you like to graph the phases of the moon and the number of crimes in your town over a five year period? Do more crimes occur at one phase of the moon than at any other? It might be possible to make a projection for the number of crimes that will occur at the next full moon.

Your information will come from a variety of sources, depending upon the nature of the survey. Let's take another example. Suppose you wanted to determine what has happened to the dog population in your town over the last ten years. You could determine this by knowing the number of licenses issued each year. The place to go for this information is City Hall or wherever dog licenses are issued. If, when the licenses are issued, the breed of dog is also recorded, then it would be possible to determine the number of animals of any particular breed. You could compare the number of German Shepherds to the number of Fox Terriers over the past ten years or longer. By graphing the data that you have obtained, you may be able to predict what breed will be the most popular three years hence, if present trends continue.

No discussion of surveys would be complete without mentioning psychological surveys. As psychology courses in secondary schools gain in popularity year after year, we can expect an increase in the number of psychology projects that are submitted.

Most psychological projects deal with behavior. If the survey deals with animal behavior, then the data is collected by experimentation. However, if human behavior is examined, the data will usually come from a questionnaire. The questionnaire is given to a selected group of individuals. The answers are analyzed and become the data. For example, you might want to find out who has more fears—eighth-grade boys or eighth-grade girls. You would devise a questionnaire to answer this question and give it to a significant number of boys and girls in the eighth grade to answer. As in all scientific studies, the larger the number of subjects, the more reliable the results. Equal numbers of boys and girls should be used if at all possible.

Your questionnaire could be relatively simple. Just a list of 20 fears and the instructions to write a "Yes" or "No" next to each would do. For example,

1. Are you afraid of fire?_____

2. Are you afraid of failing mathematics?_____

3. Are you afraid of your father?_____

And so on.

A more searching type of questionnaire would ask the subject to place a "1" next to his or her greatest fear, a "2" next to the second worst fear and so on. A point system could be devised and a value given to each "1," "2," and so on. In this way, you could compare the worst fear of boys to the worst fear of girls. All the fears on your list could be rated in this manner.

Hot Tips—From Planning to Presentation

When doing any science project, never forget one important thing. Always keep in mind for whom your project is intended! Another way of saying the same thing is: Consider who will judge or grade your project. If it is for your teacher, then prepare your project with your teacher in mind. What does your teacher like? Will he or she be influenced by a bright, colorful display of pictures and artwork? Or will the number of pages you write determine the value of your report? Does your teacher believe that "The more the report weighs, the higher the grade?"

If you are doing a project for a Science Fair with a team of unknown judges in mind, then it is best to include something for everyone. Include good artwork, attractively displayed, proving that you know the scientific concepts and principles involved in your project. If you can add something creative and slightly unique to your project, you will stand a good chance of being among the winners.

If your plans are logical, arranged in proper sequence and practical, then following them to completion usually goes along fairly smoothly. Don't expect every little detail to go according to plan, as this rarely happens. Just remember, the better your plans, the easier it will be to carry them out and the more successful your project will be. Every project, be it a written report or a working model, must be planned if you want your efforts to be rewarded.

Written Reports

1. Ask your teacher what topics you will be studying in the weeks to come. Reports on these topics usually receive more credit than reports on topics of no concern to your teacher. Your report might be used in a science lesson by the teacher or you might even be asked to read your report to the class.

2. After you have decided upon your subject and title, determine how long you want your project to be. Is your teacher influenced more by quantity than quality? Often, the guidelines for length will be set by your teacher.

3. Now that the question of length is out of the way, go to the library. Consult the card file, scientific encyclopedias, reference textbooks, the vertical file and the *Reader's Guide To Periodical Literature*. Go back to Chapter 3 and recheck all the research possibilities.

4. Depending upon your topic, it might be worthwhile to write to companies, tax-free organizations and government agencies for copies of their booklets, product literature and free photographs. Usually these items will be sent to you at no cost.

5. Stop now and think! Do you really like this project? Now is the time to change plans. You may have decided to report on "Shellfish of the North Atlantic Coast," but as you read on in more and more books, you became fascinated with the "red tides." The cause of "red tides" is a population explosion of reddish-

brown phytoplankton. Now would be the time to re-think what you wanted to do—go ahead with the shell-fish report or change over to a report on "red tides."

6. Plan the physical layout of the finished report.

  a. Prepare a *cover page* that catches the eye, if you can. Besides a title, work in some art or a photograph. Does the title reflect what is in your report? Which title would you select for your report: "Where will the 'Red Tide' Strike this Year?" or "How The 'Red Tide' Affects Us"?

  b. A *table of contents* follows the cover page.

  c. At the end of your report, include a *bibliography* that lists your sources of informa-tion. Mention the author, the name of the book or magazine, and name of the publisher and the year published. Also include the volume and number of a magazine that is referred to. Make sure your sources of infor-mation are recent. Don't waste your time copying information from books published twenty years ago unless there are no other sources in the particular field. The material in old books may well be out of date and possibly inaccurate. For example, in the 1960s, BCG Vaccine was thought to be useful against tuberculosis. Today, it has been proven to be of no value against TB.

7. Make use of copying machines when you must. Copy pictures, graphs, charts, tables—anything that will either help you write your report at a future date or be used to highlight and enhance it.

8. Enclose your report in a plastic binder before you

hand it in. These binders are impressive and serve to keep your work neat and clean.

Getting Ready for the Big Day

You have made it! Everything has been completed and with a week to spare. Your display boards are ready. The lettering is neat and eye-catching and your pictures are neatly arranged. The charts and graphs are drawn in color and look as though they were made by a commercial artist. Should you sit back now, admiring your work, relaxing to await the day of the Science Fair? No! You need this time to get yourself ready for the judging and for any unexpected emergencies. Your project may be ready but you are not.

Even if the rules don't require it, it is a good idea to have five or six copies of the abstract for your project on the display table for the judges to examine and read. The abstract is a brief summary of the main points of your project. It should be on a single typed page with no strike-overs or misspelled words. In this age of typing correction paper and fluid, there is no reason for presenting sloppy looking printed material. If you can't type, ask a member of your family to do it for you. If it is impossible for you to get your work typed, then a *hand-printed* abstract will have to do.

The abstract briefly explains what you did and what you discovered. Besides providing a brief overview of your work, the abstract will arouse the interest and curiosity of the reader, whether it's a judge, teacher or interested observer at the Science Fair. If it does its job, your abstract will induce the reader to pause and examine your project with care rather than hurry on to the next entry. When the judging is over, leave the abstract on your table. I'll explain why later on in this chapter.

When the judges examine and rate your project you will be there to answer questions they may wish to ask you. The judging team can be composed of one, two or three judges, each of whom may ask you one or more questions. The number of judges varies according to the number of projects entered in the Fair and the number of judges who show up at the appointed time. The judges are volunteers recruited from the ranks of public school science teachers, college professors, research scientists and from scientific and engineering concerns. When the judging teams are organized, the officials in charge try to match the judges to the projects they are best suited to judge. A medical doctor will be asked to judge biological projects rather than student-made microcomputers. This is not always possible and it may happen that a metallurgist will be the only one available to judge projects in the Health Sciences, such as a project dealing with preventing tooth decay. Who your judge or judges will be is purely a matter of chance. Sometimes, an excellent project does not receive an award because it is overlooked simply because the judging team was not familiar with that particular branch of science. They could not recognize the excellent quality of the student's work. This frequently happens to pure research projects when they are examined by industrial engineers who are looking for a practical aspect to every project. If this should happen to you, don't let your anger and resentment get the better of you and cause you to scrap your project. Do the reverse! Enter your project in other science competitions or work on it and make it even better than it originally was. Then enter it next year. Give another group of judges the oppor- tunity to see how good your work really is.

Back to the questioning by the judges. At the usual science fair, you will be given three minutes to explain your project to the judging team. They will then ask you some questions related to the project and your de- velopment of it. A typical follow-up question might be, "What good can come from your research?" or "How does this experimental electric battery differ from the one being perfected by Gulf + Western?"

You have to be prepared to answer any and all ques- tions. Devote time before the day of the judging to prac- ticing presenting an explanation of your project to a small group of people in approximately three minutes. Use your parents, friends, teachers, anyone who will listen. Encourage them to ask you questions related to your project. Ask your science teacher or project ad- visor to ask you technical questions about your project, since these will be the kind that the judges are most likely to ask. The more practice you get in explaining your work, the more self-assured and confident you will be when the judges approach you at the Fair and you realize that "This is it!"

When the judges question you and listen to your answers, they are probing to find out whether this is really your project or if some adult did most of the work. They also are concerned with how well you understand the nature of your project or experiment and the implications of it. A few years ago, a famous medical bacteriologist was a judge at a Science Fair in a large city. While examining the projects to which he had been assigned, he was shocked and surprised to see his very own Petri dishes as part of one youngster's experiment. It turned out that the young man's father worked in the office next to the bacteriologist's laboratory and the father had asked one of the young assistants in the lab if he could borrow a few of the Petri dishes for his son's Science Fair project. The assistant allowed the boy's father to borrow the Petri dishes. Needless to say, this particular project did not win an award.

Dealing with Emergencies

A few days before the fair is the time to get your emergency repair kit ready. You have to be prepared. You can't anticipate what might go wrong as you set up your project for exhibition. Your kit should include:

1. Tools to assemble and break down your display. A screwdriver and a pair of pliers are essential.
2. Spare parts to replace anything that can get lost or broken en route to the Science Fair. For ex-

ample, bulbs, batteries, magnets, etc.

3. An electrical extension cord, if any part of your project needs electrical current.

4. Spare screws for hinges on your panels.

5. A stapler and/or some tape to attach pictures or charts that might come loose. Also, extra plastic in case the cover gets torn.

6. Include touch-up paint and a few magic markers in your emergency kit.

7. Get a few cardboard or wooden boxes to carry any plants, lamps, microscopes or models in.

Another problem that you must face and solve is getting your project from home or school to the site of the Science Fair. My advice is to have either Mother or Dad drive you and your project there. No matter who drives you there, be certain that the driver knows how long the ride will take. If the estimate is twenty minutes, plan to depart thirty minutes before the time you are supposed to set up your project. Leaving extra time for unexpected traffic delays is important. While talking about the ride to the building housing the Fair, be sure the driver also knows how to get there. Getting lost en route will be a waste of valuable time and cost you even more by making you more nervous than normal. Being late could be tragic if your project was one of the first to be judged and you weren't even in the building! It would be better to spend the money for a taxi rather than to rely upon public transportation in many large cities.

Speaking of the problem of transportation leads naturally to the question of size and weight of your project.

Usually the rules and regulations regarding size are printed upon your entry ticket. You will be told how much space you are allotted in terms of length and width. Most Fairs do not set any height limits for the displays but don't make your display boards too tall. First of all, if the boards are over three feet in height, it will be difficult for anyone except a very tall person to read and see what is near the top. Secondly, you might not be able to fit your exhibit into the family compact car. Also, a very big display will be clumsy and very heavy to carry. Lastly, if your project is too high you may not be able to get it out of the basement or your room.

Weight is another factor to be considered. Can you and your helpers carry the display or project from the car to the place where the science fair is being held? If at all possible, it is best to bring everything from the car in one trip. This will allow the maximum time for setting up. Working under the pressure of time will often result in things not going as smoothly as when there is ample time. One way to make a bulky, heavy project easier to handle and transport is to divide it into hinged sections or by using some of the methods shown and discussed in Chapter 6.

When the projects are being set up, the exhibition area is filled with noise and confusion as the entrants and their assistants scamper around looking for their assigned space and hurriedly move their equipment into the room. All projects of one category—for example, those of ninth grade students—will be in one area while those of twelfth graders will be in a different area. Some Fairs group projects by science area, so that all the earth science projects will be found in one room while the chemistry projects can be found in another room. The purpose of grouping is to make the job of the judges easier. They can see all the projects of one type in one place and thus save time. This also makes it easier for the judges to go back and take a second look at a project that had impressed them at the start. Obvious, too, is the fact that it would be unfair to compare the work of a twelve-year-old to that of someone who is seventeen. It would be impossible to compare the merits of a biology project with that of a physics experiment.

Another consideration is your appearance when you meet the judges. Wear neat, clean clothing. Casual clothes are fine. Don't look as though you haven't changed your clothes or combed your hair for the past three days. Also, it would not be wise to wear a T-shirt with a slogan on it that might give the judges the wrong impression of you: for example, one that said, "Science is harmful to all living things". In brief, let your appearance reflect the importance of the occasion. If how you look signals to the judges an "I don't care" attitude, they may think that this attitude is true of your entry as well. Now, you might think that your clothing and hair have nothing to do with your project and it should be judged solely on its scientific merits. If you believe that, theoretically you are right, but practically speaking you are wrong. The judges are educators, engineers, industrialists, scientists and human beings with likes and dislikes. They will tend to favor youngsters who reflect their concept of what a young scientist or engineer should look like.

Finally the officials of the science fair will have cleared the judging area of parents and friends who helped the entrants bring in their material. The judging will start shortly and quiet will replace noise. Be alert and ready when the judges finally come to you. Smile at them and act friendly. This is the moment you have worked long and hard for.

Whether you are an award winner or not, stay with your project after the judging, when the public viewing of the projects takes place. Have your abstracts handy for any interested person to read. Be courteous and friendly to all those who show an interest in your science project. Explain any details they may ask about and answer their questions. Listen to their comments as well as their questions. They may give you an idea for a modification of this project that next year will result in your project becoming a prize winner. You can enter the same basic project next year provided you make some changes. A chance remark by a passerby may spark an idea that will, in the future, win you one of the prestigious awards of the International Science and Engineering Fair. This fair is administered by The Science Service, 1719 N Street, NW, Washington, DC 20036. The Science Service also administers the Westinghouse Science Talent Search. Write to them and get a copy of their ISEF Newsletter. You will find it useful, since it will tell you about the winners in these competitions. The newsletter will contain other useful information as well.

When the fair is over, remove your entry when you are supposed to. If you don't you may discover that your work, into which you put so much effort, was thrown away. Don't forget this year's project can serve as the starting place for next year's project, which will be more elaborate, more mature and even more scientific. Thus improved and changed, it may bring to you all you desire in terms of fame, recognition and prestige.

CHAPTER 5

Planning and Designing Experiments

Up to now, we have talked about starting projects and experiments. At this point, let's stop and focus on those things that should not be done when carrying out a scientific investigation. Do *not* plan to use equipment that is too expensive or too complex. Don't plan to build or buy a cyclotron, cathode ray tube, laser or scanning electron microscope. Your experiment should not require apparatus for reaching extremely high or low temperatures or pressures. It's also impossible to work under sterile conditions for long periods of time at home or in your school laboratory in order to carry on recombinant DNA experiments. If your experiment does require special equipment, you and your science teacher should try to locate that equipment at a nearby college or university. Once that has been done, your school might arrange for you to use that exotic equipment at the college.

An even better arrangement is to find a local college researcher who will agree to let you conduct your experiment under his or her guidance. This often happens, especially if your experiment sounds exciting or important to the senior scientist. Before a professional researcher will take you on, he will want to review your school record and speak to your teachers. Most important will be an interview with you. At that time the scientist will determine if you have done your homework—that is, are you familiar with the equipment you expect to use? Do you know the concepts behind its operation and the safety rules to be observed? If your research involves an organism, be familiar with its anatomy and physiology, habitat and life cycle. You can really impress your potential mentor if you can bring out during the conversation that you have a good working knowledge of one particular aspect of the plant or animal you hope to deal with—for example, its respiratory anatomy and physiology in some detail.

A former student of mine traveled three hours each Saturday in order to use special equipment at a college for freezing soap bubbles. His experiment involved the forces that determine the shape of soap bubbles.

In some cases, you will not be allowed to use equipment, especially if there is an element of danger attached to its use. Suppose you wanted to experiment with zinnia seeds exposed to various amounts of radiation. You would not be allowed to use an X-ray machine, but an experienced radiation worker could do it for you. You could even ask your family physician or dentist to expose the seeds for you using his or her X-ray equipment.

Hazardous Duties

The subject of X-rays leads to the next major point in this chapter, namely, awareness of potential hazards and dangers. Conduct your experiment in as safe a manner as possible. No experiment is worth a severe burn, being poisoned or getting mangled in an explosion. Most science experiments have some small danger associated with them. The only absolutely safe projects are written reports or pictorial displays, and even then you run the risk of stapling your finger or getting a paper cut.

Your eyes are quite delicate and most important as sense organs. Just think what life would be like if you were blind! *Safety goggles* should be worn when hammering, grinding or chipping rocks or metals and when working with flames. As a general rule, wear safety glasses or goggles during all chemical experiments. While we're discussing protecting your eyes let's lay down some absolutes: *Never* look directly at infrared or ultraviolet light through a microscope. *Never* reflect sunlight from the mirror of a microscope directly into your eyes. This practice can cause serious eye damage. It would be wise to experiment with lasers at school rather than at home because of the danger of electrical shock from this equipment, as well as eye injury from looking directly at the laser beam.

Be sure to wear a laboratory apron when working with chemicals and biological agents. In addition, wear rubber gloves when washing chemical or biological glassware to prevent both cuts and contamination.

Ether, alcohol and benzene are dangerous and volatile liquids, and if you do use them, be sure the quantities are small and that you are working in a well-ventilated room away from open flames. Actually, most gases are dangerous if inhaled in high concentrations. This is true of carbon dioxide, nitrogen and inert gases such as argon and helium.

Care must be taken when you make a survey of plants near your home. Even the plants growing inside of your home can be harmful. Some of the plants that are poisonous will surprise you. Probably the only plants that are poisonous that come to mind are poison ivy, poison oak and poison sumac. Did you know that eating the twigs of a cherry tree is the same as eating cyanide and the result can be fatal? Death can even follow the eating of a narcissus or hyacinth bulb. At best, eating these bulbs will make you quite ill. A favorite at Christmastime is the poinsettia plant. Eating a single leaf can kill you. The same is true for eating any part of the azalea. There are many other plants that are poisonous, so don't assume that if it is not mentioned here it must be "safe" to eat or chew. A comprehensive list can be gotten free from the National Safety Council, 444 Michigan Avenue North, Chicago, Illinois 60611. (Listing or showing hazardous plants could make a good project. See how easy it is to come up with ideas?)

I haven't discussed any precautions to be taken when handling bacteria or poisonous chemicals. Nor have I mentioned cuts from glassware, burns, explosions, asphyxiation from noxious fumes, electrical shock or radiation from radioactive sources. A complete list of the hazards you may encounter during science experimentation and the necessary precautions to be taken are beyond the scope of this book. There are many publications on science safety, including the *Manual of Laboratory Safety* published by the Fischer Scientific Company of New York and *Chemical Safety Guides* which is put out by the Manufacturing Chemists Association. Both of these organizations are located in Washington, DC.

My last caution deals with living animals, since many young people like to do biological experiments. The Westinghouse Science Talent Search and a number of other Science Fairs and competitions bar the use of vertebrate animals in experiments. The only exception is a survey of animals in their natural habitat. You are better off starting with invertebrates such as insects, worms or spiders in your experiment. It is harder to shift to these animals after you have started with higher life forms such as fish, frogs, reptiles, birds or mammals.

As a science educator and as a former Science Fair judge, nothing turns me off more than seeing a cruel and needless animal experiment like "What changes take place when a gerbil is starved?" or "What happens when a mouse strikes the earth after being rocketed 100 feet into space?" Experiments like these add nothing to the body of scientific knowledge. Furthermore, they have forced many science expositions and competitions to prohibit the use of vertebrate animals. This had to be done to protect both the animals and the public from viewing these "un-scientific" experiments.

To sum up, write out and discuss your experiment with your teacher or science supervisor before starting it. Focus on your personal safety, the practicality of the experiment and, if an animal is involved, that the experiment be humane.

Summary Notes

What form should your experimental design take? Your objective is to tell exactly what you hope to discover and how you plan to go about making that discovery. Your design should allow anyone who reads it to understand what you are going to do, what data you expect to collect and what procedures will be used for measuring the data. Your experimental design should make it possible for anyone who follows your recipe to carry out your experiment—to get the same or similar results.

There is a difference between the experimental design and a research paper. The experimental design is included in a research paper, but the paper contains much more, including the background readings you had done and your results and conclusions. The design for an experiment is thought out before doing the experiment, while the research paper is really a final report of your experimentation.

Research papers are divided into a number of specific sections that are arranged in a logical order and follow each other in step-wise fashion.

The first part is the *hypothesis*. We can think of the word hypothesis as a statement the accuracy of which is to be investigated or tested by the scientific method. Just to refresh your memory, by *scientific method* we mean establishing experimental and control groups. Both groups are exactly the same except for one variable. Every other factor is kept as alike as is humanly possible. "The effect of weak magnetic fields on the reproduction of Stentor" or "Extracting water efficiently from gasoline" are just two examples of hypotheses.

Secondly, you should indicate what information or clues you found in *a search of significant literature*. If your hypothesis was "Adaptations that allow Phragmites (reed-grass) to grow in salt-rich soils," then your significant readings would include botany books and specialized books on grasses. You would read all the research articles on phragmites that you could locate, as well as articles of the injurious effects of salt upon other grasses. It would be useful too to read up on the anatomy and physiology of phragmites and of other grasses, particularly on the transport system.

Next, you would explain how you plan to *test your hypothesis*. This is your experimental design in detail. One of the major weaknesses that many embryonic scientists make in designing their experiment is to use too few subjects in their experimental and control groups.

The larger the sample in both groups, the more accurate your data and your conclusions will be. A high school senior used 60 earthworms in each group in a learning experiment. Her results were much more valid than if she had used only six in the experimental and control groups.

A second weakness is the hope and desire to get positive results. Your design should not be biased. The desire to discover a significant scientific fact is very strong, even among professional researchers. Every experimenter must make a conscious effort to conduct the experiment fairly and to be sure that the conclusions reached do agree with the data. Keep in mind that negative results are just as valid and impcrtant as positive results. They may not be as dramatic, but scientifically they are just as meaningful!

Sometimes, the results are not only negative but unexpected as well. A fire injured some trees in a wooded area near your home. You did a survey that compared the growth of the surviving trees to similar trees that were not damaged by the fire. You expected to find that the injured trees grow at a lesser rate than their unaffected fellow trees. Measurements of leaf size and number revealed that the scorched trees grew much better than the others of the same species in that region. This surprise might be the starting point for another experiment—to find out why. Were harmful insects living under the bark killed by the heat?

Something else to keep in mind is how long your experiment will take. A five year period of observation and study of insect populations or air pollution in an area would not be practical if you wanted to complete it while in high school. An experiment that would take several months to complete would be much more practical.

How do you plan to *make measurements* and *collect data*? A notebook is essential to record your observations. All entries should be dated and, if helpful, the time of day should be recorded as well. If, during the course of an experiment, some unusual event occurs that seems unrelated to the experiment, be sure to note that strange happening in detail. It is possible that the unusual event may be directly related to your experiment and may suggest an experiment more exciting and important than the one you had originally planned.

This happens again and again! William Perkin wanted to make synthetic quinine from coal tar products because the French Society of Pharmacy was willing to pay a handsome reward to the chemist who could discover this procedure. Perkin got nowhere with quinine, but when he was cleaning his test tubes that held the messy coal tar with alcohol, he discovered the first important artificial dye. That dye was aniline purple. Neither he nor anyone else has been able to produce quinine synthetically, but fortunately there are other synthetic compounds that produce the same effects.

Most likely nothing earth-shaking or unexpected will take place in your experiment. Regardless, you must record your experimental information in a notebook that is used solely for that purpose. Don't use your notebook from economics class for recording your observations. Write your entries so you can read them three months later. This means they should not be too small or indecipherible! It is wise to make your entries as soon as possible. If you delay, some of the details may be forgotten.

Most likely your data will be in the form of measurements taken over a period of time at definite intervals. You can't just say that the experimental snails grew faster and larger than the controls, or that the reaction went to completion at a lower temperature when the experimental catalyst was added. You must be accurate and precise!

Should you record the snail's growth increase as 3 mm, 2.6 mm or 2.68 mm? The answer depends on several things. How accurate is your measuring tool? What degree of accuracy do you need for your experiment? If you are using a metric ruler that shows both centimeters and millimeters, it might be possible to estimate 2.6 mm, but with most rulers it would be impossible to record 2.68 mm. You would be on firmest ground by reporting 3 mm.

Suppose you are measuring crystal size under the microscope and each crystal measured between 100 and 103 microns. Should you record 101.7 microns, 101 microns or just 100 microns? Since a micron is 1/1000th of a millimeter, there is no need for tenths of a micron to be used.

If your data is in the form of drawings, 35 mm photographic slides or photographs, either the regular type or Polaroid, make sure you can identify each visual. An easy way to do this is by describing each picture in your record book. Polaroid pictures are the easiest—just write the date, time and a brief description on the back.

Your notebook is filled with entries and measurements. The experiment is over and the time has come to *organize your data into meaningful form.*

Tables are very useful and are easy to set up. Graphs

Table #1

		Counts Per Minute
Shield	1	1547
Thickness	2	1489
(mm)	3	1253
	4	917
	5	741
	6	388
	7	95
	8	12
	9	0

Graph #1

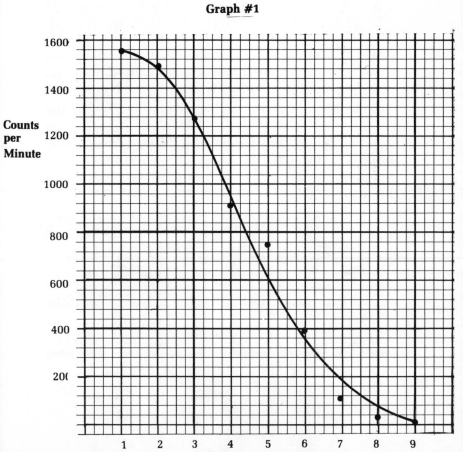

Shield Thickness (mm)

on the other hand can present some problems, but these can be overcome with a little planning and thought. Let's say that your experiment dealt with the absorption of alpha particles by an experimental absorbing material of different thicknesses. Your data would consist of the thickness of the shield and the counts per minute recorded on the Geiger counter. The data is summarized in Table 1.

In setting up the scale for your graph, select convenient figures to work with. The thickness presents no problem, since each sample is 1 mm thicker than the previous sample. The counts per minute run from zero to a little more than 1500. We want to select a scale that will tend to fill the graph and also be convenient to work with. By using a scale of 40 cpm for each vertical line and three horizontal lines for each millimeter of thickness, the graph is adequately filled and the cpm can be recorded without too much trouble.

It is better to draw a smooth curve. Don't be concerned if you don't go through each and every point. On graph 1, the curve only goes through five points. Compare graph A to graph B. Notice that the number

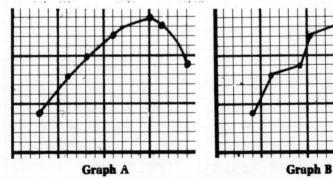

Graph A   **Graph B**

Table #2

		Counts Per Minute
Shield	1	92147
Thickness	2	64438
(mm)	3	38218
	4	14947
	5	5386
	6	1921
	7	1546
	8	1489
	9	1253
	10	1036

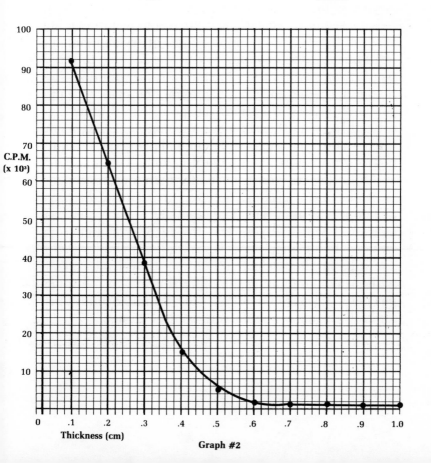

Graph #2

of points on each graph is the same, but the way the lines are drawn make a big difference.

Another student who did a similar experiment with a different kind of shielding material gathered data shown in Table 2 and Graph 2. Again, note how the graph is filled and a smooth curve is drawn.

The next step, after our data is arranged and tabulated, is to *analyze the data* or make sense of it. Sometimes you have a great deal of data and you have to find a way to deal with the many measurements. Once the data is manageable, it becomes understandable. The answer is the use of *statistics*.

Let's see how we can put statistics to use in making sense of the data collected in an imaginary experiment. Let's imagine that a young researcher decided to spray pea flowers with a 5% Gibberellic Acid solution. The researcher believed that by spraying the peas with the Gibberellic Acid Solution, the peas would grow significantly larger than in a control sample. Like Gregor Mendel, the young experimenter had many pea (Pisum) plants growing in his backyard garden. Two hundred and fifty flowers were selected for both the experimental and control groups. Between five and eight peas developed in each pod. The diameter of each pea was measured with calipers and the results tabulated as well as being recorded. Since the Gibberellic Acid could be applied selectively to one flower on a plant without contaminating the other flowers on the same pea plant, it was relatively easy to get similar conditions for both the experimental and control groups.

DIAMETER OF PEAS (mm)

NO. OF PEAS	3	4	5	6	7	8	9	10	11	12	13	14	15	16	17
CONTROL	1	4	7	8	11	43	98	382	497	508	213	149	27		
EXPERIMENTAL			2	7	19	75	92	239	303	461	556	232	116	14	6

If you graph the data according to the hints suggested a few paragraphs ago, the graph will look like this:

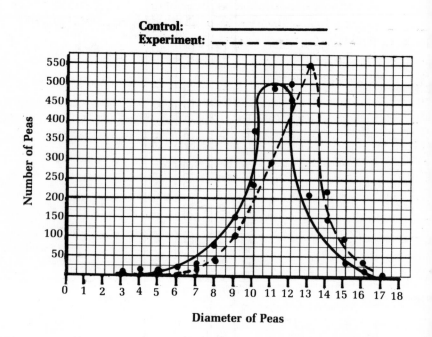

Diameter of Peas

When you look at both graphs plotted on the same sheet of graph paper, the first thing that strikes your eye is that most of the peas will be in the middle of the graph. Both graphs show fewer peas at either end. Both graphs are "Bell-shaped curves of Normal Distribution." This type of curve is to be expected when dealing with characteristics such as size, weight and so on of living things.

We also see that the experimental curve is shifted to the right of the control group. This is an indication that the experimental peas were larger in diameter than the control peas. Observe, too, that the experimental group peaks higher as well as to the right of the peak for the control group. This is another indication that the experimental peas were larger.

Stat City

Let's turn to statistics and find out how a statistical analysis compares to our visual determinations. The average diameter is called the *arithmetic mean*. This is found by adding up all the diameters and dividing by the number of measurements. The arithmetic mean for the control group is 11.3; for the experimental group it is 12.1.

The *median* is a type of average also. This is the middle measurement. There are equal numbers of measurements above and below the median. The control median is 11 while the experimental one is 12.

Still another type of average is the *mode*, which is the diameter that occurs more than any other. The control mode is 12; the experimental mode is 13.

You now have three ways to summarize the average

measurement, but you don't know how widely the measurements vary. A measure of variability tells the experimenter how widely or close together the measurements are distributed. One way to measure variability is to determine the *standard deviation*. If this is small, say 2 or 3, all the measurements are close together. If the standard deviation is around 20, then the measurements will vary greatly. The standard deviation is found by first determining the mean. Then each measurement is taken and compared to the mean. Its difference from the mean is recorded and then squared. The squares are totaled and divided by the number of measurements minus one. The square root of this figure is the standard deviation. The mathematical formula for the standard deviation is

$$\sqrt{\frac{n \ (\text{deviations from the mean})^2}{n-1}}$$

Where n is the number of measurements.

Standard Deviation: Control = 1.6; Experimental = 1.8

This means that the average pea varies plus or minus 1.6 mm from the mean diameter of 11.3 mm for the control group and plus or minus 1.8 mm for the experimental peas.

There are many other statistical studies that can be applied to your data. Some are the Chi Square (goodness-of-fit) test, frequency, linear correlation, Standard Error and so on. There are many fine books on statistics and how to use them; just look through what your library has and start with what you can understand.

Finale

When it comes to *drawing conclusions*, you would be wise to proceed with caution! Let's see why! You have completed all phases of your experiment except for the conclusion. You have spent time, a lot of thought and effort, plus aggravation and possibly even some frustration and now you are ready for the big moment. You and every other researcher wants to discover some significant scientific fact or concept. This wish is only natural; unfortunately, it rarely happens.

What you must do is to examine your data objectively and carefully. Try to remove yourself emotionally from the research project. Professional scientists try to eliminate the "personal factor" by using a number of associates. Each associate carries out one phase of the experiment. They are working in the dark. Not only do they not know what their colleagues are doing—they don't even know what the director of the project hopes to discover. In this way, each member of the research team is working "blind" and thus can report their results much more objectively.

What you must not do is to "read" an invalid, startling conclusion from your data. Even if the results are not what you want or expect, it is your obligation to report them honestly. A young woman noticed damage to sugar maple trees near her house caused by salt placed on the icy roads in the winter. She experimented with an absorbing compound that bound up the salt and prevented it from dehydrating the sugar maples.

All this researcher could conclude is that the compound prevented salt damage to sugar maple trees. She could not conclude from her experiment that it would work with equal success on eastern white pine trees or balsam firs.

The above is true if your experimental and control groups are small. For example, in the sugar maple experiment, if only two trees were treated with the absorbing compound and two similar trees were used as controls, her results would have to be termed as *tentative*. There is nothing wrong with reporting tentative results subject to further in-depth study.

Also, you have to watch out when you start using statistics. With a slanted choice of numbers, you can fool yourself in a lot of ways. Try these questions on for size: Can volcanic eruptions in the northwestern United States cause record-breaking temperatures in the southwest? Is the sale of soda the cause of an increase in vandalism?

The answer to both of these questions can be "yes"...statistically speaking!

Two events that occur in the same time frame can be shown by statistics to be related. Consider that the volcano erupting may change local weather conditions and even conditions across a broad belt of the United States. But weather moves with the prevailing winds, from west to east. Thus, since the southwest isn't in the path of the volcano's gases, its abnormal weather could not be scientifically related to the volcano. Scientists must search for another cause of the prolonged hot weather. In the summertime, more cans of soda are sold than in the cooler months—for obvious reasons. Also in the summer, people who commit acts of vandalism have warmer, nicer weather and so have more opportunities to get into mischief. The point is, just because two events occur at the same time does not necessarily prove a cause and effect relationship.

In an experiment with either plants or animals, are you sure that the experimental group did not receive slightly better food, light or living conditions? Or maybe just a tiny bit better care? If you did favor the experimental group over the control, your experiment is biased and your conclusions become invalid. One of the ways a scientist checks on his conclusions is by repeating his experiment from the beginning several times. This is a luxury that few student scientists can afford. Another check is to have other scientists repeat your experiment. Naturally, their results and yours should agree. Your best assurance of accuracy is just to follow the experimental method as rigorously as you can, checking and rechecking yourself and your procedures every step of the way.

CHAPTER 6

The Little Things Make a Project Outstanding!

If you're not ready to attempt a scientific experiment, there are a lot of projects that you can do that will impress your judges. But if you do try a pictorial display, a report, model or other static display, there are a great many things that you can do that will keep the judges from saying "This is a *nice* project, but not a great one." Those little touches, the special details, are what this chapter is all about.

Pictorial Displays

Since pictorial displays are favorites of mine, we'll start there. Let's suppose you have a topic and have already collected the pictures you plan to use. The following hints should be of help to you.

When gathering visuals for your display, don't think just of pictures. Charts, graphs, maps and drawings, even cartoons as well as pictures, will add variety to your display. Be sure, though, that they have some relevance to the topic you're explaining. Some projects are hurt because the student/experimenters throw in everything they can find.

Color is better than black and white. This is true for pictures, titles, labels, printed messages and so on. Don't forget to use a colorful background if you can. You only get one chance at the judges, so you have to catch their eye.

Planning Conference

Trim your pictures and make your work as neat as possible. An excellent way to get started is to lay out your pictures on a table or on the floor. Arrange them as you think they should be placed. Try a few different

A Bar Graph

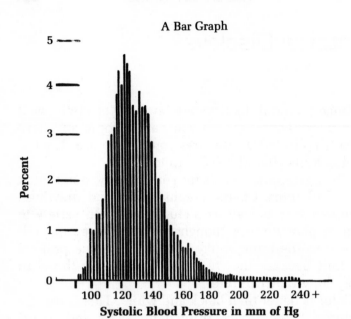

Systolic Blood Pressure in mm of Hg

A Line Graph: note the use of the solid and dashed lines.

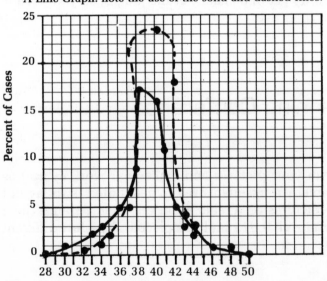

Gestation Length (Weeks)

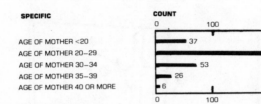

GROUP	DISORDER	FREQUENCY
White	cystic fibrosis	1/2500
Blacks	Sickle-cell disease	1/625
Greeks	B-Thalassemia	1/729
Jews (Ashk.)	Tay-Sachs	1/2900
Anglo-Saxon	Neural Tube Defects	1/220

A TABLE

SPECIFIC

COUNT

AGE OF MOTHER <20 — 37
AGE OF MOTHER 20–29 — 198
AGE OF MOTHER 30–34 — 53
AGE OF MOTHER 35–39 — 26
AGE OF MOTHER 40 OR MORE — 6

ANOTHER TYPE OF BAR GRAPH

arrangements. Select the one that pleases you the most. If your pictures trace the history of a scientific development—say rocketry—place the picture of the earliest development on the left. To the right of it, place the picture of the next development, and so on. End with the most modern rocket on the right. For other themes, such as "Active Volcanos in the World Today," place the most attention-getting picture in the center, then arrange the less spectacular pictures around it.

Decide how big you want your project to be. Science Fairs usually set a size limit on projects entered in the fair. If your project is large, with many pictures, it may be easier to work with if you divide it into two parts. If that is the case, prepare two sheets of background material (plywood, cardboard, brightly colored art board) for your display. When the two halves are placed side by side, the display will be complete.

If you glue a piece of wood to the center edge of the left and right halves of your display, you can hold them firmly together with a "C" clamp, as shown in the diagram below.

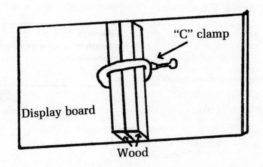

The number of pictures you plan to use should help determine the size of your display. If you plan to use six 3– by 5–inch photographs, you should *not* attach them to a piece of plywood that measures three feet wide by three feet long.

Another way to plan your display is on paper. Graph paper is very useful for this purpose because you can draw everything to scale. Indicate where each picture will be positioned. Sketch in the title also. Don't forget to mark where your labels and written explanations will be and how much room they will take up.

Background Information

Decide on your background material early. Should you use thick cardboard covered with construction paper or just oaktag? Plywood, clear plastic, pegboard— all these make excellent backgrounds for your pictorial display, but you should consider cost, availability and what you like the looks of.

Your background sheets will have to be supported in some way if they are going to be exhibited ôn a table. Two common methods of support are making an easel or using blocks of wood with grooves in them.

EASEL

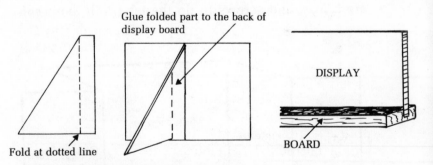

Glue folded part to the back of display board

Fold at dotted line

DISPLAY

BOARD

One of the easiest background boards to use can be made by cutting away the front, top and bottom of a cardboard box. That leaves you with a structure that has a large central panel and two smaller wing panels.

Another method that allows you to get a lot into a small space is a large piece of cardboard folded as

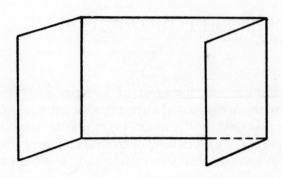

shown below. You can do the same thing with plywood or pegboard if you are handy with tools. All you need are hinges and screws to do the job. Both these con-

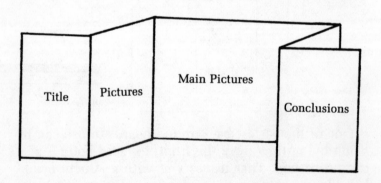

structions have several advantages: they are easy to fold, carry and set up; they give you a lot of display area in a small space and they are easily made to look organized and professional.

If a single panel is all you need, two cardboard tubes from a roll of aluminum foil or plastic wrap make excellent supports. Make a slit the length of each tube and insert your pictorial display. It may be necessary to secure your display in place by using small pieces of tape or several drops of glue.

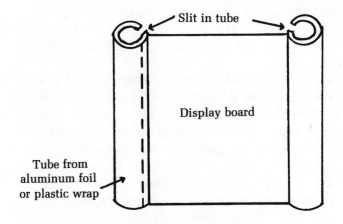

If your project has a number of objects as well as pictures that need to be displayed, you want to use pegboard. With pegboard, you can place inserts in the holes and make shelves or hang your display item. You can exhibit actual specimens, small models or other three-dimensional objects on these shelves or hung from the inserts.

Letter Perfect

How do you want your labels and written material to look? Should you print the words directly on the background, or would it be better to type them and then paste the little pieces of paper on your background board? There is a wide variety of ways you can write up your display material. You can use stencils and paints or magic markers, but that can be very time-consuming. And if you do make a mistake, there's simply nothing to do but start over. Typing your labels and written material may be very neat, but the judges and viewers will certainly have to get close to the labels to read them. Another method that is neat and simple besides is to use what is called Prestype®. These are sheets of letters, all the same size and style, that can be rubbed off a sheet and transferred onto your display board or little pieces of board that you attach to your display. It's like making words up out of those rub-off tattoos that you used to get out of bubble gum machines, except that here you're creating professional-looking display materials. These sheets can be purchased at almost any stationery store for about $3–6 a sheet, and one sheet should be enough to complete almost any display. These are details that you must decide! Don't be afraid to discuss these details with your parents or friends with artistic talents. They can help you make these decisions.

Final Touches

How are you going to attach the pictures to the background? This may seem like a minor detail, but it happens to be important. Transparent tape is a better choice than staples—for obvious reasons. But glues are even better. Avoid the use of glues that leave ripples in the paper after they dry. Test the glue on a piece of scrap paper that is the same as that which you plan to use to make sure that it dries smooth.

It's a good idea to cover your display with clear plastic when it is completed to keep fingerprints and such off it. The type of plastic your mother uses for wrapping left-over food is fine for this purpose or sheets of the inexpensive plastic that builders use to cover freshly poured concrete is good too.

You may discover that your display is to be exhibited in a poorly lighted place. If there is an electrical outlet nearby, it is worthwhile for you to bring one or two lamps from home in order to illuminate your exhibit. This is particularly important if your display is in a Science Fair and the judges are coming to view and judge your entry. Try placing the lights in different positions in order to get the best possible effect.

Written Projects

Written reports are also effective grade-getters. One of the first things you should do is ask your teacher what topics your class will be studying in the weeks to come. Reports on these topics will usually receive higher grades than reports on topics that are of no interest to your teacher. It is even possible that your teacher will use your report in a science lesson or ask you to read your report to the class. Even if your report just sits on the teacher's desk, you're going to have the advantage of understanding more about the lesson because you've done independent research into it.

After you've asked your teacher what the class will be studying, your next step is to head for the library. When you get there, talk to the librarian. Librarians are *always* ready to help people learn to use the library. These experts can help you locate the books, periodicals, journals, pamphlets or maps that you'll need to get the information you're seeking for a well-written, up-to-date report. For more information on how to use a library see Chapter 3, "Literary Sources."

Another excellent source for information is people working in the field you want to report on. Don't be afraid to write companies, corporations or government agencies for information. They're only too happy to send you booklets, pamphlets or letters explaining what they're doing and what they've discovered. And, almost all this information will be sent to you free of charge. For example, if you're working on a report on energy, you should drop a line to several oil companies, the

U.S. Department of Energy, a few coal companies and maybe even one of the companies that make nuclear reactors, like Babcock & Wilcox. You can find all these addresses by looking in one of the many listings of corporations—the *Standard and Poor's Directory of American Corporations*, for example.

One warning—when you look things up at the library, make sure that your sources of information are recent. Don't waste time on information from books published twenty years ago. That information is very likely out-of-date and possibly incorrect. For example, in the 1960s BCG vaccine was thought to be very useful against tuberculosis. Today, it is known to be of no value. So, check the copyright date of the books that you use. The copyright will be on the title page or on the page just after the title.

There are some small touches that can improve your presentation immensely. First, you should have an eye-catching cover page that includes your title, your name and a picture or illustration, if possible. A table of contents should follow the cover page. And, at the end of the report, you should include a bibliography that lists your sources of information. The bibliography entries should include the name of the author, the title of the book or magazine article from which you took your information, the name of the magazine, the city it was published in, the name of the publisher and the year of publication. There is a proper form for this and if you wish to follow it exactly, check your English grammar book or *Words Into Type*, a grammar/style book (back to the library).

Make sure that your report looks neat. Enclose it in a plastic binder before you turn it in. Get some illustrations. Use copying machines if you must. Copy pictures, graphs, charts, tables—anything that will highlight your report.

Models

If you decide a model is what you would like to make for a science project, then the hints that follow may make your time and efforts worthwhile.

1. Draw a picture of what you plan to build. If possible, draw your picture to scale on graph paper. Go to the library and find out everything you can about what you're building. Then use the pictures, diagrams and information you've gathered to put together your drawings.

2. Decide how large you want your model to be.

3. List the materials and tools that you will need in order to make your model.

4. Show and discuss your plans with your parents or other knowledgable adults who are good at working with tools. They will tell you if your project is practical. They may help you with the difficult parts, saving you time and avoiding costly mistakes. Occasionally a youngster's

project ends up being the work of Dad or Uncle Jim, with the child providing only the basic idea. Personally, I don't see anything wrong with an interested parent or relative providing guidance and help. But you should do the planning and most of the work.

5. When your project has been completed and the wood or metal has been sanded or filed smooth, the addition of paints will make your handiwork more pleasing to the eye. If you are working with clay, purchase different color clays in order to make your model more attractive. Be sure to note on your preliminary sketch (hint #1) what colors you will use and where they will go.

6. Prepare your labels and title with care; try to be as neat as possible.

7. If it is necessary, attach your model to a firm base made of plaster of paris or plywood in order to keep it upright.

8. If your model tells a scientific or technological story, be sure that the story is clear to all who view it. A brief written or typed statement, attached to the model's base, may be all that is necessary.

Working Models

There is very little difference between a working model and a stationary model. The only additions to the tips mentioned above are:

1. When building your working model, *Follow directions no matter what!* This is true when building a store-bought kit, or following the directions in an article in a magazine such as *Popular Science*, or even if you are working with plans from a reference book.

2. Try to put your model up against a suitable background. Read the tips mentioned earlier in this chapter for setting up a pictorial display.

Terrariums and Aquariums

There are many projects or experiments that can be carried out in a terrarium or aquarium, but if you are using a twenty gallon tank or terrarium, don't plan on carrying it to school or elsewhere. However, there is nothing to prevent you from taking pictures of your project and preparing a pictorial display. Besides the obvious problem of moving a large glass container full of water, remember that saltwater aquaria are very delicate environments. They're hard to get started and they are difficult to maintain. So, once yours is established, don't risk upsetting the delicate balances of light, temperature, and so on by trying to move it.

Freshwater aquaria are much simpler to start and maintain if you follow a few simple rules. First, thoroughly wash the gravel you plan to use under running water. Use enough gravel to cover the bottom to a depth of at least 5 centimeters. Then, fill the tank with clear pond water. If this is unavailable, use tap water that has been standing in an open jar for at least a day. This gets rid of the chlorine.

Place your freshwater aquarium where it will get its light from the north or from the east, unless you plan to use *fluorescent* lamps. Wait until the water is perfectly clear before adding plants or animal life. Plants are not really necessary. Oxygen is absorbed from the surface of the water, provided the water is exposed to the air. However, plants *do* absorb carbon dioxide while carrying on photosynthesis. This will permit more oxygen to be absorbed.

If you want plants, the best rooted plants to use are vallisneria or sagittaria. Root them in the gravel—soil is not necessary. Elodea (Anacharis) and cabomba are excellent floating plants.

Terrariums

Besides the common desert *terrarium* of sand and such, the Woodland Bog ranks as another favorite. In order to make the Bog type terrarium, you should place a layer of gravel or small stones on the bottom of a glass terrarium. Then, add approximately 5 cm of acid soil (a mixture of peat moss and vermiculite).

Place a layer of sphagnum moss (5 cm thick) on top of the acid soil, and then anchor your plants in the soil and water thoroughly but not excessively.

Keep your terrarium at room temperature. Place it where it will receive light from the north. Direct sunlight will be harmful since it will cause the temperature to rise too high for your plants to survive. Ideal plants for the bog terrarium are ferns, sundews, Venus flytraps and pitcher plants.

Science Survey

If you plan to do a *Science Survey* as your project, your data can be presented as a written report or as a visual display with graphs, tables and charts as the main atttractions. If you present a report, your introduction, which should follow the title page or table of contents, will explain how you got involved in this survey or what importance it has to your education or class, to the rest of the world or all of the above. This should be followed by your data and a brief statement on how it was collected.

Summarize your data in the form of tables, charts and graphs to make the survey easy to understand. Your conclusions, drawn from the data, should be logical and reasonable. And, when using the written report format, be sure to add several pictures or diagrams to make it more attractive.

CHAPTER 7

Experimental Authority

Once your experiment is completed, you will have to switch roles and become a scientific author. There is no single, set way to write up your research paper. The *abstract*, a statement that is a brief digest of your procedure, results and conclusions, may be placed directly after the title or at the end of your paper, just before the bibliography.

One thing that everyone agrees upon is the only way to start is with the *title* and your *name* on a cover sheet. The title tells the reader what the experiment is about—for example, "Determining the Number of Isomers of Organic Compounds as a Function of the Number of Carbon Atoms" or "The Direct Effects of Atrazine on Zea Mays (Corn)."

The preference here is to place the abstract after the

title. The abstract gives the reader an overview of what to expect when reading the entire paper. More important, a well-written abstract will arouse interest in the mind of the scientific reader and motivate him or her to read further. Carefully read the abstract below. Observe that there are three paragraphs. The first is a short statement of introduction. The second deals with the procedure, while the last vaguely infers what conclusions were reached. Notice that the wording tends to make the reader curious and want to clarify what "far more sensitive" really means.

THE COMPARISON OF BIOLOGICAL AND IMMUNOLOCHEMICAL METHODS FOR THE IDENTIFICATION OF THE PRESENCE OF HERPES SIMPLEX ANTIBODIES

During viral infection, all mammals manufacture antibodies against the invading organism. In this study, three methods of identification of Herpes simplex antibodies were examined and compared. The virus used was Herpes simplex virus, which is quite common and infects human beings. Thus, most people have antibodies against this virus.

The three methods compared in this study were: determination of neutralizing antibodies, enzyme linked immunospecific assay and crossed immunoelectrophoresis. Determination of neutralizing antibodies is a well-known biological method. Recently, a number of highly sensitive immunochemical procedures have been developed. Among these are the enzyme-linked immunospecific assay and the crossed immunoelectrophoresis.

The result of this experiment shows that all three methods gave similar results but the newer methods were far more sensitive and could provide more infor-

mation on how the antibodies reacted with the Herpes
simplex virus proteins.

In the *introduction*, you should tell the reader why
you selected this as your experiment. The background
of the experiment should also be discussed in this section. This means you should mention the historical
background that led up to your experiment and the
important literary references you examined. It is always
wise to mention those researchers who came before
you. One way to do this is by writing, "Meyers and
Ternes (4) reported that the percentage of...." The (4)
refers to the fact that Meyers and Ternes are the fourth
entry in your bibliography.

The experimental *procedure* follows the introduction. Has your mother ever gotten a recipe for a particularly delicious cake from a friend and discovered that
she could not bake it anything like her friend does?
Most likely, her friend gave your mother an inexact
recipe. She may have told your mother, "Stir milk and
flour until the batter is thick enough. Add a little salt
and enough orange flavoring to get the color just right."
Your mother could not make the cake properly because
the directions were not specific. Don't do what your
mother's friend did when you write up your experiment.

Tell exactly what you did. Don't say: "I placed a few
drops of zinc chloride solution...." Say: "I placed 5 ml
of .5N solution of zinc chloride." Write what equipment
you used and every step of your procedure in the correct
order. Detail the characteristics of your experimental
and control groups.

In 1804, N. Th. De Saussure wrote in his paper, entitled "On the Influence of Carbonic Acid Gas on Mature Plants," the following procedure: "Out of carbonic acid gas and ordinary air shown by a gas burette to contain 21/100 oxygen, I made up an artificial atmosphere which occupied 5.746 liters. Lime water showed it to contain 7½% of carbonic acid gas...." Even in the early 1800s, scientists were aware of the need to report their experimental procedure with precision.

Next in order will be your *observations*. Place your tables, charts, graphs, diagrams and photographs in this section. Your wording and use of language in this portion of your report will be determined to a large degree by the nature of your investigation. In some cases, your statements will not be precise, while in others your observations will be definite and exact. Consider these two statements taken from two different experimental papers.

> "Ion microphotographs indicated that calcium was plentiful in the cell walls. Potassium was absent from the cell walls, but abundant in the vacuoles."

> "The angular diameter of X-rays emitted from Cassiopeia A is 5 minutes of arc as seen through the X-ray telescope."

In the first case, it is impossible to tell how much calcium and potassium are present in the microphotograph with any degree of accuracy. The writer uses such terms as "absent," "abundant" and "plentiful." In the second case, the author is quite definite because of the nature of the instrument used in making his observations.

Besides reporting your results, you are expected at this point in your paper to analyze them. This will become clearer after looking at a few sample statements that analyze the data. "It is likely from our data that the 2^+ calcium ion in most plant tissue is mainly stationary" is one example. Another is, "The results in Table #1 show that sodium transport is strongly inhibited by adding 10^{-3} Ouabain." "As shown in Figure #2, the subpolar North Atlantic at the midpoint of ice growth during the stage 5 transition was within $1-2$ C. of today's values" would be a third.

Logically, the researcher will draw *conclusions* after analyzing the data. Here again, wording is important and will be related to the type of experiment that was carried out. A few sample conclusions can serve as models to illustrate this point.

On the basis of the calculations, I can conclude that the bright areas of X-ray emission are regions of high gas density.

It is quite clear that the condition and quality of the wasps is much lower for those without honey.

The evidence indicates that both ions have a high affinity for binding calcium.

The fact that nalxone did not stimulate the optic receptors of the grasshoppers suggests that vision is not involved in this type of behavior.

Our evidence contradicts the theory that cooler waters upwelling at the equator causes sea-ice growth.

Don't be afraid to use terms such as *tends to, indicates* or *suggests* rather than terms like *is the cause of, will always result in* or *must*. Besides stating conclusions, it is only fair for you to mention your *experimental limitations*, especially if your conclusions were stated in conditional terms. Your concluding section should also contain some sentences that explain the significance and any possible applications that you can think of that result from the conclusions. Let's look at some typical statements taken from research papers.

> It would be interesting to determine whether the results obtained for grasshoppers apply to other animal species.
>
> The first use of the ion microscope for the study of plant tissue is encouraging and further applications should be made.
>
> Further study of young supernova remnants will enable scientists to examine the precise nature of interstellar gas.

The last of your writing will be to list all of your references in your *bibliography*. Your references should be listed, by author, in alphabetical order. Don't feel that because it is placed last that the bibliography is unimportant. This section of your paper allows you to give credit to those scientists whose work in earlier times served as the basis for your research. Repeating what was mentioned earlier in this book, books are cited by author, title, publisher, place of publication and year. Mention, too, the specific pages you read, unless, of course, the whole book was devoted to your topic. Magazine articles should be listed by author, title of the article, name of the periodical, volume number, date of issue of the particular issue and the pages that the article appeared upon. For example:

Cosmovivi, C. B. *Supernovae and Supernova Remnants*. Hingham, MA: D. Reidel Publishing Co., 1975.

Culhane, J. L. *Vistas in Astronomy*, Vol. XIX, Part I, pp. 174–213. Elmsford, NY: Pergamon Press, Inc., 1975.

Gorenstein, P. *New Frontiers in Astronomy*, pp. 58–67. San Francisco: W. H. Freeman & Co., 1970.

Shkovsky, I. S. *Supernovae*. New York: Wiley-Interscience, 1968.

Woltjer, L. "Supernova Remnants." *Annual Review of Astronomy and Astrophysics*, Vol. 10 (1972), pp. 129–158.

Your research paper should be typed and double-spaced. Use only one side of the paper. Have adequate margins at the top, bottom and sides. Besides arranging your typing neatly, make sure that you have not misspelled any words and that your grammar and punctuation are acceptable. Since your paper will be read by other scientists who are familiar with your topic, there is no need to avoid the use of technical terms. Naturally, in a report that you plan to read to your classmates, either simplify the language or explain any technical language that you may use.

CHAPTER 8

Biological and Ecological Cafeteria

Welcome to a cafeteria-style presentation of biological and ecological experiments and projects! In a food cafeteria you can select one of many appetizers, main courses and desserts. The selections of foods are wide and varied. In this cafeteria, you can select an *organism*, a *variable* and an *interaction*. The end result is not a meal but a scientific project or experiment. You are encouraged to mix and match whatever suits your fancy. Let's see how a project can be made from the assortment of organisms, variables, and interactions.

Organism	+ Variable	+ Interaction	= Project
Spirogyra (algae)	+ Pesticide (Captan)	+ Photo-synthesis	= The effect of 2% Captan solution on the rate of photosynthesis of Spirogyra
Hydra	+ Vitamin E (nutrient)	+ Reproduction	= The effect of Vitamin E on the ability of Hydra to reproduce

It needn't be Spirogyra or Hydra—you could have used live ants or earthworms or even bread mold. The number of projects is unlimited! Don't be bound by this list. If you have a variable that sounds exciting, use it! Let your scientific curiosity lead the way.

One caution—some organisms, variables and interactions don't go together. You wouldn't put mustard on your chocolate ice cream. Nor do "Wild Flowers," "Temperature" and "Intelligence" go together in this cafeteria. Neither can you mix "Vinegar Eels," "Change of diet" and "Migration."

Biological Experiments and Projects

ORGANISMS

Algae

Anabaena
Chlamydomonus
Chlorella
Desmids
Eudorina
Nitella
Nostoc
Oedogonium
Oscillatoria
Pandorina
Protococcus
Spirogyra

Ants

Bacteria

E. coli
Nitrogen Fixing
Purple Photosynthetic

Beetles

Flour
Horned

Carnivorous Plants

Venus Fly Trap
Pitcher Plants
Sundews

Centipedes

Cockroaches

Crabs

Fiddler
Land
Sand

Crayfish

Crickets

Cyclops

Daphnia

Eggs

Brine shrimp
Chick

Flies

Dragonflies
Fruit
House
May
Stone

Flowers

Asters
Lilies
Roses
Zinnias

Hornets

Hydra

Lichens

Millipedes

Mites

Molds

Bread
Penicillin
Slime

Nematodes

Planaria

Plants—Fresh water

Cabomba
Elodea
Sagittaria
Vallisneria

Plant Parts

Flowers
Leaves
Pollen
Roots
Stems

Protozoa

Ameba
Blepharisma
Colpidium
Didinia
Euglena
Paramecium
Paranema
Spirostonium
Stentor
Volvox
Vorticella
Zoothamnium

Sea Horses

Shrimp

Brine
Fairy

Slugs

Snails
  Land
  Mud

Sowbugs

Spiders

Springtails

Vegetables
  Corn
  Oats
  Onion
  Pea
  Radishes
  Tomatoes

Vinegar Eels

Viruses
  Tobacco Mosaic
  $\left.\begin{array}{l} T_2 \\ T_4 \end{array}\right\}$ (grown in E. coli.)

Wasps

Wax Moths

Worms
  Earth
  Meal
  Sea
  White (enchytraeis)

Yeast

VARIABLES

Antibiotics

Antibodies

Antiseptics

ATP

Auxins

Chemical Ions
  CL^-, Na^+, Ca^+

Cloning

Detergents

Diet
  Change
  Substitution

Drugs

    Experimental
    Household

Disease—effects of

Enzymes

Food

    Vitamin
    Mineral
    Nutrient

Gibberellic Acid

Grafting

Hormones

Humidity

Hydroponics

Iodized Salt

Light

    Absence of
    Presence of
    Specific color
    Polarized
    Ultraviolet

Magnetism

Mutation

Neurohumors

Overcrowding

Ozone Layer

Parasites

Pesticides

pH

Pheromes

Plant tumors (Cancer)

Pollutants

    Solid
    Gaseous
    Liquid
    Noise

Pressure

Radioactive Isotopes

    I_{131}
    P_{32}

Temperature   Touch

INTERACTIONS

Adaptations   Excretion

    To environment
                               Fermentation

Bird Nests   Food Production

    Construction   Quality
    Location   Quantity
    Survey

Competition   Genetics

    Food   Inheritance
    Light
    Mates   Germination
    Space
    Water   Seeds
                                   Spores

Development   Insect Control

    Abnormal
    Normal   Intelligence

                                   Measure of
Digestion   Studies

Embryology   Learning

Endangered Species   Conditioning
                                   Habit
    Flowers   Instinct
    Insects   Memory

Life Histories

Metabolism

Migration

Natural Habitat

Nitrogen Fixation

Photosynthesis

Population Counts

Regeneration

Reproduction

Respiration

Transport

Circulation

Viability

After you have looked over the choices and combinations, you still may not be enthusiastic about any possible project. Don't despair—all is not lost! There may still be a biology project in your future. Try this! Pick an organism and live with it for awhile. Get to know it; make it a pet. As you learn more and more about the plant or animal, some question about your pet will come to mind. There you are! Your project is to get an answer to that question.

Ecological Projects and Experiments

Our approach to ecological projects and experiments will be slightly different from the one we took for the strict biological projects. Now we will have two "mix-and-match" choices rather than three.

ECOLOGICAL CONCERN	STRATEGY
Acid Rain	Alcohol
Air Pollution	Auto Exhaust Emissions
Cheap Energy	Biomass
Energy Storage	Coal
Endangered Species	Coal Gas
Geothermal Energy	Conservation
Noise Pollution	Fossil Studies
Nuclear Energy & Wastes	Gasohol
Oil Spills	Geothermal Energy
Ozone Layer	Greenhouse Effect
Photochemical Air Pollution	High Silica Glass
	Hydrogenation
Stress	Incineration
Tidal Wetlands	Methane
Waste Disposal Sites	Oil
Water Pollution	Pyrolysis
	Recycling
	Re-refining

(continued next page)

Solar Energy—Photovoltaic Conversion and Solar Thermal Conversions
Sludge
Sulfur Dioxide
Survey
Water Purification
Wind Power

Even with two columns to select from rather than three, there are many possibilities. Consider three possible projects that come to mind using the same two choices:

Ecological Concern + Strategy = Project
Cheap Energy + Gasohol = Is the production of alcohol by bacteria using non-edible plant parts (corn husks) feasible?

= Can the gasoline engine be modified to operate efficiently on a 50% gasoline–50% alcohol mixture?

= Can alcohol be chemically converted to a more efficient fuel?

You see that there are many projects that can be devised from the lists above. The same caution holds true that not every ecological concern and strategy can go together. *Waste Disposal Sites* and *Auto Exhaust* are an example. My last caution is that you should not limit yourself to the items on these lists. These are just starting places, so don't be afraid to add to either or both lists!

CHAPTER 9

Physical Sciences Cafeteria

This is very similar to the previous cafeteria. You can again select from two choices: Field of Study and Related Topic. If, as you go through the lists, you get the feeling that you have read some of the terms before, you are probably right. This is because the various sciences—Physics, Chemistry, Earth Sciences—can no longer be considered "pure." We speak more and more of science as being an interdisciplinary study. Ions, atoms and radioactivity are not limited to either chemistry or physics but are studied in both, and in earth science and biology as well.

FIELD OF STUDY

Acceleration   Adhesion

Airplane Wing Design

Behavior
   Gases
   Liquids
   Plastics
   Polymers

Chemistry
   Inorganic
   Organic
   Soil

Coal Dyes
   Synthetic dyes

Complex Ions
   $Co(NH_3)_6^{+++}$

Cosmology

Crystals

Design and Construction
of Devices

   Brake
   Carburetor
   Clock

Earthquakes

Electricity
   Electrochemistry
   Electromagnets
   Electrostatics

Energy

Erosion

Forces
   Centripetal
   Friction
   Gravitational

Fuels
   Enrichments

Heating
   Efficiency of fireplaces

Holography

Hurricanes

Hydrolysis

Ice Crystals

Ions & Ionization

Isomers

Mechanical Analysis of Toys
  Frisbee
  Slingshot

Metals
  Corrosion

Meteors

Minerals
  Magnesium
  Mica
  Quartz

Mining

Molecular Size

Momentum

Motion Resolution

New Products & Uses
  Amorphous Silicon

Ocean Currents

Optics

Oxidation-Reduction

Phase Change

Polymers

Pressure

Radioactivity

Refraction

Satellites
  Man-made
  Natural

Sound
  Reflection
  Speed
  Transmission

Sunspots Activity

Surface Tension

Tidal Forces
  Action

Trace Elements

Vapor Pressure

Volcanos

Wave Motion—Light

Weather

Work

RELATED TOPICS

Air Flows

Alcohol
  Solid

Analysis of NASA Data

Binary Stars

Brownian Movement

Chromatography
  Paper
  Thin-layer

Cloud Chamber

Collisions on Air Table

Cooling Curves

Diffraction

Digital Linear Circuits

Doppler Effect

Electrical Resistance

Electromagnets

Electron Beam

Esters

Fibers
  Natural
  Optical
  Synthetic

Flame Tests

Force Vectors

Geiger Counters

Heat Flow
  Insulation

Indicators

Ion-exchange Resins

Kinetic Studies

Decomposition
Oxidation

Laser Beams

Machines
  Simple

Magnets

Microscopes

Mineral Deposits

Newton's Laws

Opto-acoustic Effect

Orbits of Planets

pH

Photoelectric Cell

Photography

Qualitative Analysis

Reflection

Solutions

Smoke Tunnels

Sun Dials

Synthetic Rubber
  Butyl Rubber
  Neoprene

Telescope

Tracking
  Solar Bodies

Thermoplastics

Topography

Water
  Films
  Hard
  Removal from Fuels

Wave Height

Wind Mills

This list is by no means complete. It is a starting place for you to use. Be imaginative in your selections.

CHAPTER 10

Some More Sources

You can get ideas for projects and experiments from what you read in the newspapers and magazines or from what you see and hear on television and radio. These sources usually don't give you enough information in order to proceed. So, it would pay you to get more information in order to determine if a project or experiment is realistic for you; that is, if it is within your abilities and resources to carry it out.

When you hear or read that a particular company or university is doing something scientifically that excites you, don't be afraid to search out further information. For example, if you had read the article in the February 1980 issue of *Scientific American* by Mary K. Wicksten on decorator crabs, and something in the article was unclear or raised a question, you would have to go further. Your first step would be to read the bibliography for that article. The bibliography is located on the last page. If you examined these sources, and they proved to be of no help, then you would have to take the next step. In the section of the magazine entitled "About the Authors," you would find out that Professor Wicksten was working at the University of Southern California. Hopefully, by writing your specific question to her, she would respond and resolve the issue for you.

During your search for a project, read not only the articles in the magazine or journal, but examine the advertisements as well. In that same February 1980 issue of *Scientific American*, General Motors placed an ad that dealt with oxygen molecule dissociation on platinum. The advertisement discussed the fact that Dr. John Gland, their Senior Researcher, was in charge of basic surface chemistry of catalysis. If this field sounded appealing to you, further investigation, including a well-written, intelligent letter to Dr. Gland, would result in a response either from him or a member of his group.

Another ad in that same magazine describes the very thin solar cells being developed by the Hughes Aircraft Co. of Culver City, California. If working with solar cells of this type seemed like a possible project, then writing to that company might very well result in learning further details.

Suppose you read in your local newspaper that the scientists at TAFA Metallisation, Inc. had chanced upon a strange aluminum alloy that had all the characteristics of metals except that it rapidly dissolved in water. This discovery could have sparked the thought of building a flood alarm using this new alloy. The first problem would be to locate the company since its address was not stated in the newspaper article.

You could call the newspaper and they might be able to help you. A better way would be to go to the reference desk of your town library and ask for the *Thomas Register of American Manufacturers*. This reference lists the name, address and telephone number of all the manufacturing companies in the United States in alphabetical order.

Other possible library reference sources that should be in your local library are *Moody's Industrial Manual* and *Standard & Poor's Register of Corporations*. From any of these sources you would learn that TAFA Metallisation, Inc. is located in Bow, New Hampshire.

Let's take a look at other places that you can write to for information on specific topics and also general information. Many companies and United States governmental agencies are quite proud of their research and development teams' projects. Thus, they have published many explanatory booklets and magazines. Since they are interested in maintaining good public relations, their scientists and engineers will usually cooperate and answer specific questions asked by young, potential scientists. However, if you write and say, "I need a project by Wednesday on X-ray diffraction. Please tell me one that I can get completed by then"...forget it! This type of inquiry will not be answered.

Get on the mailing list of the United States Superintendent of Documents, Government Printing Office, Washington, DC 20402. Periodically you will be sent a brochure that lists recent government publications on

a wide variety of topics, including science and technology. The publications offered for sale are at reasonable prices and can prove very helpful in preparing all
sorts of reports. All of the booklets are prepared by
various governmental agencies. Sometimes it pays to
write to the specific agency for a list of their publications. Possibly the particular agency may send you a
single copy free of charge. The addresses of some agencies that might be helpful in doing science projects and
experiments are:

Dep't of Agriculture Research Service
Beltsville, MD 20705 (Growing plants and insect
control)

National Aeronautics & Space Administration
Jet Propulsion Laboratory
California Institute of Technology
Pasadena, CA 91103 (Booklets contain excellent,
unique pictures of planets taken during Voyager
and Viking missions)

National Oceanic and Atmospheric
Administration
U.S. Department of Commerce
11420 Rockville Pike
Rockville, MD 20852 (Booklets and pamphlets
on violent storms and related topics)

Public Health Service
U.S. Department of Health, Education & Welfare
Rockville, MD 20857. (Publications on disease and
health such as sickle cell anemia)

Your neighborhood or town library gets a monthly catalog of all publications sold by the U.S. Government Printing Office. Their catalog is much more complete than the thin brochure that is sent to those on the mailing list.

The National Air & Space Museum of the Smithsonian Institution, Washington DC 20560, publishes an excellent pamphlet entitled "Air & Space." The articles and news briefs deal with space travel, airplanes and related topics such as parachutes. Check with your science teacher. He or she may already be on their mailing list.

The National Energy Foundation, 366 Madison Ave., New York, NY 10017 coordinates the efforts of many corporations concerned with energy. The Foundation organizes and administers SEER (which stands for Student Exposition on Energy Resources). The Exposition consists of student projects related to energy conservation and the energy crunch. SEER competitions are held in a number of states, usually during the month of May. The National Energy Foundation has published a number of booklets devoted to the winners, complete with abstracts of their projects. The booklets are illustrated and you can see how others have displayed their work. If you are thinking of doing an energy-related project, the booklets just mentioned will prove to be very helpful. Your science teacher should be able to provide copies of current SEER material.

If an energy project sounds interesting to you, try writing to your local gas and electric company or to:

Energy Conservation Research
9 Birch Road
Malvern, PA 19355

National Coal Association
Director of Educational Services
1130 17th St. NW
Washington, DC 20036

Edison Electric Institute
Public Relations Dept.
1111 19th St. NW
Washington, DC 20036

Atomic Industrial Forum
Publications Office
7101 Wisconsin Ave.
Bethesda, MD 20014

American Petroleum Institute
Public Relations
2101 L St. NW
Washington, DC 20037

National Petroleum Council
Director of Information
1625 K Street NW
Washington, DC 20006

American Ventilation Association
P.O. Box 7464
Houston, TX 77008

Speaking of energy, nuclear energy experiments for students are outlined in a free booklet provided by the Thomas Alva Edison Foundation, 18280 West 10 Mile

Road, Southfield, MI 48075. The experiments are relatively simple and safe, employing low limits of alpha and gamma rays.

Publications from the American Chemical Manufacturers Association, 1825 Connecticut Ave. NW, Washington, DC 20009, include laboratory safety guides as well as ideas for projects and experiments.

Most of the large companies prepare booklets on their products for their stockholders and for the general public. The companies are very happy to send you these booklets because it is a form of advertising for them and the booklets improve their public image because they show how the company's products improve the quality of life for all of us. You could use these booklets and magazines as starting places for projects, particularly a pictorial display since the illustrations are outstanding.

Three such companies are:

Monsanto (Chemical) Company
800 North Lindberg Blvd.
St. Louis, MO 63166

International Business Machines Corporation
Old Orchard Road
Armonk, NY 10504

E. I. duPont de Nemours & Co.
Wilmington, DE 19898

All of the names and addresses of the large manufacturing companies can be found in the *Thomas Register*, *Standard & Poors* or in *Moody's Manual*.

The Millipore Corporation, Bedford, MA 01730, has

initiated a Millipore Projects Program. Most of the projects involve the detection of bacteria from lake or river water. Their literature is free and contains complete instructions, using Millipore equipment.

Scientific supply house catalogs can be used to get ideas for projects and experiments. The catalogs will also give you a good idea of the costs involved. Just a few examples are:

Carolina Biological Supply Co.
Burlington, NC 27215

Connecticut Valley Biological Supply Co.
Valley Road
Southhampton, MA 01703

Lab-Aids Inc.
130 Wilbur Place
Bohemia, NY 11716

Macmillian Science Co.
8200 South Hoyne Ave.
Chicago, IL 60620

Nasco Biologic
Fort Atkinson, WI 53538

Sargent-Welch Scientific Co.
7300 North Linden Ave.
Skokie, IL 60076

Wards Natural Science Establishment
P.O. Box 1712
Rochester, NY 14603

Lastly, if animals are of interest to you, write to the Animal Welfare Institute, P.O. Box 3650, Washington,

DC 20007. They have booklets that have ideas for humane biological projects. Another possible source is the National Society for Medical Research, 1029 Vermont Ave. NW, Washington, DC 20005.

Index